Text by Adele Evans
Edited by Alex Knights and John Mapps
Series Editor: Tony Halliday

CITTÀ DI TORINO

turismo
Torino

Berlitz POCKET GUIDE

Turin

First Edition 2005

PHOTOGRAPHY
All photography is courtesy of Turismo Torino, except SIPA Press/Rex Features 11, 85; Chris Coe 13, 28; AKG London 16; The Art Archive 18; Alex Knights 3TR, 47; CuboImages srl/Alamy 73; Amos Schliack/ ABPL 98

CONTACTING THE EDITORS
Every effort has been made to provide accurate information in this publication, but changes are inevitable. The publisher cannot be responsible for any resulting loss, inconvenience or injury. We would appreciate it if readers would call our attention to any errors or outdated information by contacting Berlitz Publishing, PO Box 7910, London SE1 1WE, England. Fax: (44) 20 7403 0290; e-mail: berlitz@apaguide.co.uk www.berlitzpublishing.com

➤ **Don't miss the Museo Nazionale del Cinema (page 51), a temple to the art of filmmaking**

Built in the 18th-century Castello di Rivoli (page 63) is home to a very contemporary collection of artworks ▲

The Egyptian Museum in Turin (page 44) is the most important of its kind outside Cairo ◄

TOP TEN ATTRACTIONS

Expansive Piazza Castello (page 23) is the baroque heart of Savoy Turin ▼

◀ In the home of Martini, it's no surprise that the social highlight of the day is *aperitivo* hour (page 104)

Overlooking the city is the Basilica di Superga (page 58), an architectural masterpiece housing the tomb of the Savoy royal family ▶

A former Fiat factory, Lingotto (page 61) holds shops, hotels, a gallery and cinema, topped by an elevated test track ▼

▶ Wander the narrow streets of the lively Quadrilatero Romano (page 30)

Piedmont's idyllic winelands (page 68) are dotted with forts ▶

Sestriere (page 78) is a smart skiing resort in the Via Lattea, or Milky Way ▶

CONTENTS

A ➤ in the text denotes a highly recommended sight

Fact Sheets

INTRODUCTION

Turin, capital of the Piedmont region, is changing. No longer is it defined by the fortunes of Fiat or seen as a northern industrial city worth only a fleeting glimpse on the way to other better-loved Italian slices of *la dolce vita*; nor is its fame restricted to its status as the home of the most venerated piece of cloth in Christendom. If these were your preconceptions of Turin, you may be surprised. Stimulated by the prestige of playing host to the 2006 Winter Olympic Games, the city has smartened up its streets and piazzas, polished to perfection its array of historical and cultural treasures, and laid out the welcome mat for visitors, Italian and non-Italian alike. If this is not enough to convince you, the exquisite locally made chocolate, world-famous Torinese vermouth and distinctive Piedmontese cuisine should all tip the balance in Turin's favour.

Mouthwatering *giandulotti*

Distinguished Heritage

The Romans knew a good location when they saw one – in this case, a strategically poised spot between the Alps and the Ligurian Sea. When the House of Savoy eventually made this settlement their capital in the mid-16th century, they had a well-planned Roman town upon which to build. And build they did: palaces, baroque castles and churches, harmonious piazzas and sweeping boulevards graced the city centre.

Turin is a spiritual home for lovers of coffee and chocolate

Lavish royal hunting lodges and pleasure palaces were constructed in the hills and parkland surrounding the city.

In 1861, Turin was made the first capital of the Kingdom of Italy, and its aristocratic, elegant demeanour reflected this prestige. Chandeliers twinkled in the marbled, mirrored cafés, where discussions and plans had made the Unification of Italy into a reality. An impressive 18km (11 miles) of gracious, colonnaded walkways protected royalty and commoner alike from the elements.

> **Renowned for their good taste, the Torinesi are allergic to ostentatious displays of wealth. While Turin is the biggest market in Italy for French fashion designer Hermès, any purchases made there will be discreetly packaged in a plain white, unmarked bag – the only Hermès shop in Europe that doesn't advertise its own brand. Other designer stores, such as Armani, are very successful here, but the Versace shop had to close – perhaps a little too flashy for this city.**

City of Culture

Although four years later, the Savoys moved out of the Palazzo Reale – a shift that heralded a new era of industrialisation – they left behind a formidable legacy of art and culture, perhaps most apparent in the city's proliferation of museums and galleries. Turin's Egyptian Museum is in fact the world's second-largest collection of Egyptian art and artefacts after that in Cairo. And the Savoys' art collection, showcased in the Galleria Sabauda, contains outstanding old masters. Outside the city, the gracious lines of the 18th-century palace, Castello di Rivoli, conceal Turin's contemporary art gallery. And, high on the roof of the old Fiat factory in the city's Lingotto district, is the futuristic *scrigno*, or jewel-box, designed by architect Renzo Piano. The treasures inside form the collection donated to the city by the late

Giovanni Agnelli (the Godfather of Fiat) and his wife
Marella – some 25 masterpieces including works by Matisse, Picasso and Renoir.

Italy's National Museum of Cinema is housed in the Mole
Antonelliana, long the symbol of Turin and the world's
tallest museum. True to its status as the birthplace of the
Italian film industry and its enduring love affair with that
medium, the city today has a higher proportion of cinema
screens to inhabitants than any other in Italy. Culture in the
city extends to ballet, opera, music and theatre too, with
works staged year-round in centuries-old and state-of-the-
art auditoria.

Beyond the City

The city's dramatic backdrop of the snow-capped Alps is a reminder that part-and-parcel of Turin's allure for contemporary

Turin's skyline is framed by the Alps

visitors are the attractions of its easily accessible hinterland of alpine resorts, including Sestriere (the Alps' first purpose-built ski resort), and its enticing cluster of wine-producing towns and villages.

The hills of the Langhe and Monferrato produce some of the world's most celebrated wines, such as Barolo and Barbaresco, while the villages of Asti and Alba are famed for their respective connections with the sweet, sparkling Asti Spumante and Piedmontese 'white gold'; the latter, a delicious white truffle, is just one of the ingredients of the local gourmet cuisine.

Not far away is the source of another luxury product, the 'Cashmere Valley' of Biella, from where most European designers source their fabrics. Tradition meets 21st-century laser design in the textile mills found here.

Made in Turin

While Turin is perhaps synonymous with the Fiat Group, founded here in 1899, the city also leads the field in aeronautics and aerospace (Alenia, Avio, Microtecnica) and telecommunication (Motorola, Telecom Italia).

The Torinese have also been pioneers in the field of food and drink. Those crispy bread sticks, *grissini*, which grace every Italian table, were first made in Turin. Chocolate assumed its modern form here when, in 1678, Madama Reale Giovanna Battista Disavoir Nemours authorised and regulated its production. Turin's love of hazelnut and chocolate confectionery has become famous under the Nutella brand. As for drinks, Vermouth was invented here in 1786 by Benedetto Carpano, and the city is home to such names as Lavazza, Marchesi di Barolo and Martini & Rossi. Piedmont continues this tradition of being at the forefront of gastronomic innovation as the home of the Slow Food Movement.

The region also has a long tradition in textiles. Famous brands such as Zegna, Loro Piana, Agnona and Cerruti produce prized fabrics.

Turin puts the 'T' in Fiat

At the Cutting Edge

The flair for innovation and design has always been part of the Torinese character. Whether it's the automobile, cinema, television, telecommunication or fashion industries, this is where they were developed and continue to develop. As Turin moves ever forwards, brand new, state-of-the-art railway and metro systems are under construction: 15km (9 miles) of underground tracks are being put down and industrial wasteland is being reclaimed. The city is also a working base for some of the world's most important architects, such as Gae Aulenti, Norman Foster, Massimiliano Fuksas, Arata Isozaki, Jean Nouvel and Renzo Piano.

Whether you think of this city as the home of the Savoys, the much-analysed Holy Shroud, the Fiat car or the Juventus football team, Turin continues to reinvent itself. In addition, its hills, parks and gardens make it one of the greenest cities in Europe. Prepare to be pleasantly surprised.

A BRIEF HISTORY

First traces of Palaeolithic Neanderthal civilisation in the region are estimated to date back to 68,000BC. Much later, between 500–400BC, there is evidence that a tribe of Ligurian Celts and Gallic races, known as the Taurini, made their settlement, Taurasia, at the confluence of the rivers Po and Dora. When Hannibal passed through this area en route to the Alps with his elephants in 218BC, the Taurini put up great resistance. But, after a siege of three days, Taurasia was razed to the ground.

Little was then heard of the place until the 1st century BC. Julius Caesar recognised the area's strategic importance as a gateway to the Western Alps and an important crossroads on the way to Gaul. In 58BC he founded an important military colony here, Colonia Giulia. Thirty years later, under the rule of the Emperor Augustus, the settlement was renamed Augusta Taurinorum. Augustus rebuilt it in the form of an enclosed rectangle divided into 72 blocks (insulae). In common with the usual Roman grid layout, its roads ran east–west and north–south. The city had four gates and 6-m- (19½-ft-) high surrounding walls. The *decumanus maximus* (main east–west road) survives in the layout of the present-day Via Garibaldi, and the remains of the walls, Palatine Gate and Palatine Towers are still visible.

> **The Taurini took their name from a Celtic word for tower or mountain. The word's similarity to the Latin *taurus* gave rise to the city's symbol – the bull.**

House of Savoy

After the fall of the Roman Empire in the 4th century AD, Piedmont fell prey successively to Barbarians, Burgundians,

Lombards and Franks. Charlemagne then took control and it was subject to his empire until the Carolingian line died out in the late 9th century.

The House of Savoy was founded by Umberto I Biancamano (Umberto the White-handed) in the early 11th century. It was through the marriage of Countess Adelaide to Umberto's son, Count Oddone of Savoy, that Turin and the surrounding area became increasingly important. This was her third marriage and she brought with her strategic lands on both sides of the Alps. Eventually Turin came under the influence of the Savoy family who were granted the feudal lordship by the Emperor Frederick II in 1248. By 1280 the House of Savoy controlled the whole region under Tommaso III.

The Savoys ruled Turin from their capital of Chambéry (now in France) until 1536 when the city was seized by King François I of France. Duke Emanuele Filiberto of Savoy

The much modified Palazzo Madama dates from the 13th century

won the city back in 1557 after victory at the Battle of San Quintino and the subsequent Treaty of Cateau-Cambrésis, which returned the duchy to the Savoys. Seven years later Emanuele Filiberto, known as Testa 'd Fer (Iron Head) – a reference to his clever military strategy – ordered the construction of the Mastio della Cittadella to fortify the city. He also transferred the capital of the dukedom from Chambéry to Turin and brought back the Turin Shroud from Chambéry.

Capital of Savoy

For two centuries Turin and the surrounding region of Piedmont developed as one of the most influential centres of the Italian peninsula. The dukes of Savoy expressed their power, wealth and taste by commissioning grand projects from the age's best architects and artists.

Under Carlo Emanuele I (1580–1630), the Palazzo Reale was given a new façade by Amedeo di Castellamonte, while Ascanio Vitozzi designed the Porta Nuova area and the Piazza Castello. During the 17th and 18th centuries Turin became the creative centre of baroque architecture in Europe. Two of the most eminent baroque architects, Guarino

---

Baroque Turin

Guarino Guarini (1624–83) from Modena was primarily an architect of churches. His trademark lofty domes are visible in his Church of San Lorenzo and the Chapel of the Holy Shroud. But he also designed the Accademia delle Scienze and the Palazzo Carignano, whose flowing, curved brick façade is a masterpiece. He was succeeded as royal architect by Sicilian Filippo Juvarra (1678–1736), who applied his more classical French-style master strokes to the stunning west façade of the Palazzo Madama, the royal hunting lodge at Stupinigi and the Basilica of Superga – among many others.

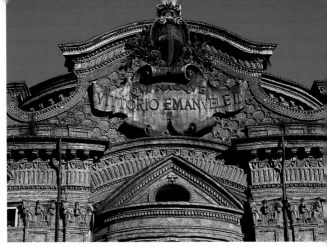

Guarino Guarini's baroque masterpiece, Palazzo Carignano

Guarini and Filippo Juvarra, built magnificent churches, palaces and royal residences.

The War of Spanish Succession, fought between Spain and her rival European powers, ushered in great changes for Turin and her rulers. In 1706 Turin, an ally of Austria, found itself under siege by Franco-Spanish forces. Local miner Pietro Micca blew up the underground tunnels beneath the Citadel to break the siege, becoming a hero in the process. The house of Savoy did well from the subsequent Treaty of Utrecht (1713). Vittorio Amedeo II was granted Sicily (the island was exchanged for Sardinia in 1720) and the title of king. There followed a peaceful period until the end of the 18th century.

Then in 1798 the Savoys were forced into exile in Sardinia as Napoleon marched his troops into Piedmont. Under the French, Turin began to undergo a metamorphosis from fortress into a monumental city, full of wide, tree-lined

Austrian defeat at the Battle of Solferino in 1859

streets. Military buildings were replaced with civic facilities and city walls were dismantled. After the collapse of the Napoleonic regime in 1814, the Savoy ruler Vittorio Emanuele I was returned to the throne.

Towards the Risorgimento

The 19th century saw an escalating liberal movement in Europe and a campaign to unify the various states of Italy. Turin played an important role in both movements.

Liberal uprisings in 1821 led to Vittorio Emanuele's abdication in favour of his brother, Carlo Felice, who created city landmarks such as Piazza Carlo Felice, Vittorio Emanuele – now Vittorio Veneto – and Emanuele Filiberto – now della Repubblica. Carlo Alberto I who succeeded him earned the nickname 'King Ditherer' – *il re tentenna* – because he eschewed decisions of state in favour of the arts and sciences. He was no match for the reformers of the era, of whom Count Camillo Benso di Cavour was the greatest. In 1848 Cavour published his liberal *Statuto Albertino* advocating an independent constitution and a two-chamber parliament. Carlo Alberto granted the Statute, but went on to declare a disastrous war against the Austrians, who ruled much of northern Italy. He abdicated shortly after his defeat at Custoza in 1848, in favour of his son Vittorio Emanuele II.

Cavour, Vittorio Emanuele's prime minister, played a leading role in the Risorgimento – the movement for Italian unification. His diplomatic efforts to unite the northern Italian states resulted in Napoleon III declaring war on Austria. With the help of the great freedom-fighter Giuseppe Garibaldi, the Austrian Emperor Franz Josef II's armies were routed at the battles of Solferino and Magenta. The treaty that Austria was forced to sign in 1859 surrendered all of Lombardy and the ducal territories of Modena and Parma to Piedmont. And, in 1861, the Kingdom of Italy was declared with Turin as its capital and, as its first king, Vittorio Emanuele II .

The Kingdom of Italy

Although Turin lost its position as capital to Florence in 1865 (Rome finally became capital in 1871), this period was one of pride and jubilation, which saw the creation of bold nationalistic architecture in the city. Wide, Parisian-style boulevards,

From 1852 until his death, it was Count Camillo Benso di Cavour who was Italy's true political leader. He fervently believed in Italian unity and independence, through the leadership of Piedmont, the strongest state. With the help of Giuseppe Garibaldi he achieved partial unification of Italy and was appointed Italy's first prime minister under King Vittorio Emanuele II in 1861. He died just four months later. The complete unification of Italy was finally achieved in 1870.

large squares such as Piazza Vittorio Veneto, parks, gardens and bridges were created during this time. The tallest brick building in the world when it was constructed, the Mole Antonelliana put Turin into the vanguard of international cities of art. Neoclassicism replaced the baroque, master-minded by Juvarra's successor, Benedetto Alfieri.

As industrialisation gathered pace, population growth accelerated, almost doubling from 250,000 to 415,000 between 1881 and 1911. In 1884 Turin hosted the General Italian Exhibition for which the Medieval Village in the Valentino park was built. Italy's motor industry came into being during this crucial period, with the founding of the Fabbrica Italiana Automobili Torino (FIAT) in 1899 and Lancia in 1909. Olivetti – another business destined to become a household name – came into being in 1908. Turin became the birthplace of Italian cinema in 1904.

One of many successful brands to emerge from Turin

Early 20th Century

Despite being on the winning side in World War I, Italy faced political and economic crises in the immediate postwar era. Turin was a hotbed of left-wing activism, and strikes were common. The Communist Party came into being in 1921 under the leadership of Turin's Antonio Gramsci, who warned against the growing Fascist movement. Left-wing resistance to Fascism was very strong in northern Italy, but when the *fascisti* marched on Rome in 1922, King Vittorio Emanuele III invited their leader, Benito Mussolini (Il Duce), to form a government. Gramsci was arrested in 1926 and sentenced to 20 years' imprisonment. Committed to further industrialisation in order to

Turin car museum has a wealth of classic examples on display

bring about a self-sufficient state, Il Duce brought workers from the south to work in Piedmont's factories. In 1939 the 3,000,000 sq m Fiat factory opened in Turin's Mirafiori district – the first mass production plant in Italy.

Postwar Turin

Turin's military equipment factories were prime Allied bombing targets in World War II; the retreating Germans added to the destruction. By war's end, some 40 percent of Turin's buildings were reduced to rubble. But in the 1950s and 60s the city rose again, its population soaring as huge numbers of southern Italians made their homes here. Fiat played a central role in the city's new prosperity. At the helm of the company from 1966 was Giovanni Agnelli, grandson of Fiat's founder. Fiat became the largest corporation in Italy, and Agnelli, in the eyes of many, became the country's most powerful man.

Turin continued to be a breeding ground of radicalism. The left-wing Brigate Rosse (Red Brigade) terrorist group was born on Turin's Fiat factory floor in the 1970s. Its avowed aim

Celebrating the city's successful bid for the 2006 Winter Olympics

was to overthrow capitalist Italy by violent means. The period from 1973 to 1980 became known as the *Anni di Piombo* (years of lead) and were characterised by many terrorist attacks, especially in Bologna and Milan, but also in Turin. After a decade of terror, most of the group's leading members were in prison by the mid-1980s.

Changes were in the air by the 1980s. The iconic Lingotto factory closed in 1982 and, by the 1990s, Fiat was forced to diversify due to competition from South-east Asian car manufacturers. Giovanni Agnelli's death in 2003 seemed to symbolise the end of an era – that of Turin as 'Fiatville' – although the company retains a strong presence in the city.

A New Era

The decline in heavy industry has prompted the city to diversify. The Lingotto factory has been transformed by architect Renzo Piano into a cultural and trade centre. Service industries are starting to play a more prominent role. And the city's long-standing reputation for excellence in industrial design continues.

The choice of Turin to host the Winter Olympic Games in 2006 has given the city a whole new international visibility. A number of ambitious projects have been built or are in progress, including a new railway system and metro, as well as state-of-the-art sports facilities.

Historical Landmarks

68,000BC First traces of Neanderthals in the area.

500–400BC The Taurini, descendants of Ligurian-Celts and Gallic races, settle along the Po.

218BC Taurasia, founded by the Taurini, destroyed by Hannibal.

58BC Julius Caesar founds Roman military colony, Colonia Giulia, here.

28BC Colonia Giulia renamed Augusta Taurinorum.

400–773 Barbarians, Burgundians, then Lombards rule.

773 Charlemagne defeats the Lombards.

888 Turin becomes part of Frankish King Berengario's kingdom.

1248 Granted in fief by Frederick II to Thomas II of Savoy.

1536 Turin and most of the duchy seized by François I of France.

1559 Treaty of Cateau-Cambresis restores Savoys' territories to Duke Emanuele Filiberto.

1564 Emanuele Filiberto transfers capital of the dukedom of Savoy from Chambéry to Turin.

1580–1630 Baroque architecture flourishes under Carlo Emanuele I.

1706 Turin under French siege.

1713 Treaty of Utrecht; Vittorio Amedeo II is made king.

1798 Under Napoleon, French troops occupy Turin. Piedmont annexed to France after Napoleon's victory at Marengo in 1800.

1815 Napoleon defeated at Waterloo and Turin returned to Savoy dukes.

1861 Kingdom of Italy declared, with Vittorio Emanuele II as king and Turin as capital.

1899 Fiat (Fabbrica Italiana Automobili di Torino) is founded.

1920 Birth of Italy's Communist party (PCI) under Antonio Gramsci.

1945 Liberation of Turin; city left devastated by bombs.

1973–80 *Anni di Piombo* (years of lead) – terrorist attacks from left-wing Brigate Rosse group.

2000 Display of the Holy Shroud for jubilee year; Fiat forced to sell off non-core assets.

2003 Death of Fiat boss Giovanni Agnelli.

2006 Turin hosts Winter Olympic Games.

WHERE TO GO

Central Turin takes its rectangular shape from the plan of the Roman encampment from which the city evolved. The compact nature of this area makes it perfect for strolling around. As you walk, take comfort from the knowledge that the centre's 18km (11 miles) of colonnaded walkways serve as a refuge from wet or hot weather.

This guide divides central Turin into several districts: Piazza Castello, Il Quadrilatero, Cittadella, Centro Città and, across the Po, La Collina. The major historical, cultural and architectural attractions of each are highlighted in turn. Also worthy of a visit are the Lingotto complex, the former Fiat works south of the centre, and the former royal residences on the city's outskirts. For those wishing to explore the surrounding Piedmontese countryside, including the ski resorts, the guide ends with a selection of excursions of varying lengths.

PIAZZA CASTELLO

The historic heart of baroque Turin lies in the pedestrianised **Piazza Castello**, the harmonious work of three great architects, Ascanio Vitozzi, Amedeo di Castellamonte and Filippo Juvarra. All around you are reminders of the house of Savoy, Turin's rulers for six centuries. But this is also the site of the original Roman settlement, Augusta Taurinorum, founded in the 1st century BC. The Roman centre was protected by walls and connected to the outside by four fortified passages which opened onto the major roadways. The eastern gate leading towards the River Po was known as the Porta Decumana, the area now occupied by the **Palazzo Madama** (closed for restoration until 2006).

The distinctive Mole Antonelliana pierces the city skyline

In the 14th century, a fortress on the site was rebuilt by Prince Filippo d'Acaja; further enlargement took place in the following century. In the 1600s, the fortress became the palace of Marie Christine of France, Madama Reale, who ruled as regent. But it was another Madama Reale, Maria Giovanna Battista di Savoia Nemours (widow of Carlo Emanuele II), who brought about the decisive transformation of the building. She enlisted the help of architect Filippo Juvarra to design a new western façade of the palace. The work, made entirely from Chianocco stone, was completed in 1721. 'A façade without a building' was the harsh verdict of essayist Francesco Milizia. However, it received more positive reactions from other critics who preferred it to the Louvre's façade in Paris. The building is a curious jumble of styles, but very imposing nonetheless.

Palazzo Madama

Restoration work means that access is limited, but there are free tours of the restored parts of the palazzo; tours during the week need to be booked (tel: 011-442 9912). The **Museo Civico di Arte Antica** (Museum of Ancient Art) inside Palazzo Madama is closed until 2006.

Just north of the palazzo is the royal library, **Biblioteca Reale** (open only for temporary exhibitions). This lovely, wood-panelled library contains manuscripts, drawings, photographs, maps and volumes from the Savoy and Savoy-Carignano collections – around 200,000 items. It is also home to Leonardo da Vinci's famous *Self Portrait at Sanguigna* and his *Code on the Flight of Birds*, which are occasionally exhibited and sometimes available to view on request.

Leonardo da Vinci's *Self Portrait* is housed in the Biblioteca Reale

In the same building as the library is the **Armeria Reale** (closed for restoration until late 2005; previously open Tues, Wed, Thur, Sat and Sun 1.30–7.30pm; also Wed and Fri 8.30am–noon; admission fee; tel: 011-543 889). This is one of the world's richest collections of arms and armour, with Oriental, Napoleonic and Risorgimento weapons, including 57 complete suits of armour and Duke Emanuele Filiberto's 16th-century sword. The collection also features firearms and stilettos – Italian daggers.

Outside, next to the Armeria, is a statue of Christopher Columbus. Rubbing the statue's little finger is supposed to bring good luck. The digit now gleams from the constant attention and has been replaced four times.

Palazzo Reale

Beyond, through the Piazza Reale, is one of Turin's most splendid baroque monuments, the **Palazzo Reale** (open Tues–Sun 8.30am–7.30pm; admission fee; tel: 011-436 1455). Begun in the 1640s, this was the official Savoy royal residence, modified and extended by the court's architects, Carlo and Amedeo Castellamonte, Filippo Juvarra and Pelagio Pelagi.

Although the exterior is austere, the interior drips with gold and velvet, chandeliers and chinoiserie, frescoes and tapestries. These palatial surroundings were home to the Savoy dukes and kings until 1865. The royal apartments on the first floor are set around a courtyard and include the Salone della Guardia Svizzera, once the meeting place of the Savoys' Swiss mercenary guards. There are exquisite decorations and frescoes, including the Flemish artist Jean Miel's *Allegory of Peace* fresco in the Sala del Trono (throne room). The Gabinetto Cinese is an excellent example of the 18th-century chinoiserie style, its beautiful lacquerwork designed by Filippo Juvarra. The recently restored queen's throne room is opulent in shining gold, while the *scala delle forbici* (scissor staircase) is yet another masterwork by Juvarra, created in 1720. Look for the medallion under the first flight of steps with a grotesque mask framed by a snake's forked tongue, cut by a pair of scissors. This was Juvarra's defiant message to those who believed he would never complete this work.

Outside in the grounds are the **Giardini Reali** (royal garden; open daily Oct–May 9am–5pm and June–Sept 8.30am–6.30pm), which were designed in the French style by André Le Nôtre, who also created the gardens at Versailles. Seventeenth-century statues, flowerbeds and a splendid mythological fountain by Juvarra's nephew, Simone Martinez, adorn these gardens, which, although a little run-down, are nonetheless very charming. The imposing railings at the entrance of the Palazzo Reale are said to be on the spot of the white magic heart of Turin *(see page 36)*.

Two of the city's most famous cafés are in Piazza Castello. **Baratti & Milano** at No. 29 (open Tues–Sun 8am–9pm) is a 19th-century fantasy of chandeliers and marble, little changed since it was established in 1873. It is the perfect spot for a hot chocolate or coffee accompanied by a mouthwatering pastry.

You can take away ingot-shaped boxes of the Torinese speciality, *gianduiotto*, which combines chocolate with local hazelnuts. Other specialities stocked here include *marrons glacés*, sugarcoated flower petals, delicious *arancín* (orange pieces dipped in bitter dark chocolate) and *baci di dama* ('ladies' kisses' – also made with chocolate and hazelnuts).

Much smaller, but just as atmospheric, **Mulassano** at Piazza Castello 15 (open daily 7.30am–9pm) is an excellent example of Liberty style (Italian Art Nouveau), with original furnishings in its wood-panelled interior and lovely sculpted leather

The church of San Lorenzo looks over Piazza Castello

ceiling. Its patrons once included members of the royal family and the stars of the nearby Teatro Regio. The speciality here is the *tramezzino*, a type of sandwich made with very thin slices of bread, which Mulassano popularised in the 1920s. The anchovy and pepper *tramezzini* are especially delicious and many say they are the best in Turin.

Also in Piazza Castello, beyond the porticoes, lies Turin's opera house, **Teatro Regio** (open Sat 3pm Oct–Jun, rehearsals permitting, for guided tours; tel: 011-881 5241/ 011-881 5209). The modern façade hides a long history. Originally completed in 1740, the first royal theatre was the setting for the premiere of Puccini's *La Bohème* in 1896. In

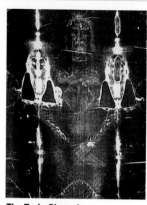

The Turin Shroud

1936 the building was engulfed by fire and further irreparable damage was caused by bombing during World War II. Today's building is one of Europe's most important modern opera houses, built and designed by the architects Marcello Zavellani-Rossi and Carlo Mollino between 1967 and 1973. Inside is the trademark Torinese brickwork and, despite a violet ceiling (considered to be bad luck for performers), the theatre has excellent acoustics and is regarded as a top-class opera and theatre venue.

Church of San Lorenzo and the Duomo

Just on the western corner with Piazza Castello at Via Palazzo di Città is the church of **San Lorenzo** (open Mon–Fri 8am–noon and 4–7pm; Sat 8am–noon and 3–7pm; Sun 9am–1pm, 3–7.15pm and 8.30–10pm). This church's plain exterior belies the beauty within – a fantasy of baroque stucco, marble, gilding and sculptures. The highlight of the octagonal interior is the superb dome designed by Guarino Guarini, opulently decorated with elegant plays of shape and volume. The church also has on view a full-size replica of the Turin Shroud (the original is in the Duomo).

Just behind San Lorenzo in Piazza San Giovanni, also known as Piazza del Duomo, is Turin's cathedral, the **Duomo di San Giovanni Battista** (open Mon–Sat 7am–noon and 3–7pm; Sun 8am–noon and 3–7pm). Dedicated to John the

Baptist, the patron saint of Turin, and built 1491–8, this is the sole example of Renaissance architecture in town. Designed by Tuscan architect Meo del Caprino, the façade is decorated with white Chianocco marble, while beside it stands a 60m (200ft) campanile built 30 years earlier, and crowned by an 18th-century bell house by Filippo Juvarra. Guarino Guarini had a hand here in the gloriously baroque octagonal cupola, built in 1694, which illuminates the black marble Cappella della Sacra Sindone (Holy Shroud chapel). However, following a devastating fire in 1997, the magnificent chapel has remained closed, although the Sacra Sindone was left unscathed. The shroud is only exhibited on rare occasions, but a copy, which is a third smaller than the original, is on view in the north side of the Duomo *(see below)*. At the northern end of the square there are remains of ancient walls, a Roman cobbled floor, a Roman theatre, and the Porta Palatina – the gateway to ancient Augusta Taurinorum.

Enshrouded in Mystery

The Shroud of Turin, known in Italy as the Sacra Sindone, is imprinted with the image of a man who has been tortured and crucified. While the faithful believe that this is the very piece of linen in which Christ's body was wrapped, others believe it is fake. Carbon dating and chemical analysis have proved inconclusive and it remains a mystery.

Brought to Turin from Chambéry in 1578 when the Savoys moved their capital, the shroud has 'miraculously' escaped theft and fire several times, most recently in 1997, when a conflagration ravaged the Duomo di San Giovanni Battista. It is now kept behind bullet-proof glass, covered in cloth, in the cathedral's left-hand transept. Last displayed to the public in 2000, the shroud's next appearance is scheduled for 2025. Despite these rare displays, it remains an object of reverence for believers and of fascination for visitors to Turin.

A narrow street in the Quadrilatero Romano

IL QUADRILATERO

The Quadrilatero Romano – or **Il Quadrilatero** for short – extends west from the Piazza Castello. This area's four-sided shape and tight network of streets are legacies of the old Roman settlement whose heart this was. With its bars, clubs and cafés, this is one of the city's liveliest neighbourhoods for nightlife. It also includes colourful markets and historic churches.

Piazza della Repubblica

Every morning the **Porta Palazzo** market (open Mon–Fri 7.30am–1pm, Sat 7.30am–7.30pm) bursts into life in the **Piazza della Repubblica**. It is a teeming mass of activity as stall-holders advertise their wares, which include everything from saucepans and shoes to pungent cheeses and exotic spices.

Just behind, north of Porta Palazzo, is a maze of streets housing **Il Balôn** flea market (open Sat 7.30am–7.30pm), which began life in the mid-19th century. Here you can find everything from second-hand and antique furniture to retro clothes and books. Every second Sunday, it expands into **Il Gran Balôn** (open 7.30am–1pm), in which 200 stallholders from the whole of Piedmont (and some from France) congregate to display their goods. Rare antiques, collectors' items, silver, carpets, jewellery, clothes, the countess's castoffs – all are for sale, along with a lot of tat – attracting large numbers of people all searching for that elusive bargain.

The streets around here are well worth exploring. They vary in nature from the gentrified to the bohemian with some good restaurants and bars. As the site of Turin's ethnic quarter, this is a buzzing, colourful and exotic place.

Piazza della Consolata

Heading south from Piazza della Repubblica, which was laid out by Filippo Juvarra, there are more echoes of the baroque in the Torinesi's favourite church in Piazza della Consolata, **Santuario della Consolata** (open daily 6.30am–12.30pm and 3–7.30pm). Known simply as La Consolata, its origins go back to the 10th century, although all that remains of the original Romanesque church are the 11th-century bell tower, Turin's oldest, and some fragments of the apse. Most of what you see today dates from the 1670s (by Guarini) and the early 18th century (by Juvarra), making this one of the city's

Turin's flea market, Il Balôn

most splendid examples of the baroque. Among its treasures are Guarini's soaring, frescoed dome and Juvarra's glorious altar. Dedicated to Maria Consolatrice (Mary the Comforter and protector of Turin), the church contains a gallery housing a collection of ex voto gold and silver hearts and paintings representing miracles credited to the Virgin. Some are childlike, graphic paintings of car accidents, others show people restored to health.

For a change of pace, try the café **Al Bicerin**, opposite the church. Opened in 1763, the café was much loved by important politicians, nobles and intellectuals of the Risorgimento, including Count Cavour, the Italian unification movement's main architect. The philosopher Friedrich Nietzsche was a frequent visitor, and the writer Alexandre Dumas mentioned Al Bicerin as being 'among the good and pleasant things of the city' during his stay in Turin in 1852. Today, this is a great spot to enjoy the delicious Torinese *bicerin (see below)*.

The Capital of Chocolate

Chocolate, a substance believed to be the drink of the gods by the Aztecs, arrived in Europe through the Spanish conquistadores, thence to Italy through its links with Spain. Originally the privilege of the House of Savoy, chocolate became popularised by ducal decree in 1678. Since then, Turin has been the capital of Italian chocolate and a number of celebrated chocolate treats have been dreamt up by the Torinese.

Beloved of children at Easter, the chocolate-filled egg originated in Turin when Signora Giambone hit upon the idea of filling hens' eggs with liquid chocolate in 1725. The heavenly chocolate-and-hazelnut confection, *gianduiotto*, was invented by the Caffarel-Prochet company in 1867 and named after the Torinese carnival mask, Gianduja. Turin is also home to a sure contender for the drink of the gods – *bicerin* – an uplifting mixture of hot chocolate, espresso and cream.

A short walk south towards Via Garibaldi leads to Via San Domenico and the church of **San Domenico**, (open daily 7am–noon and 4–6.30pm), home to Turin's oldest frescoes. Restored in 2003, the fresco cycle dates from 1360 and is attributed to Maestro di San Domenico. Dating from the 13th century, the church is also the only example of the

Church of San Domenico

Gothic style in Turin, although susbstantial rebuilding took place in the 18th century. On display is a flag from the Battle of Lepanto of 1571, when a combined Spanish and Italian fleet defeated that of the Turks. It depicts a bull – symbol of Turin and the crown.

Piazza Corpus Domini

South of the Piazza della Consolata is the **Piazza Corpus Domini**, site of the ancient Roman forum. A fruit-and-vegetable market has been held here since the 14th century. Today's market, of organic produce and handicrafts, takes place on the first Sunday of the month in front of the Town Hall. In the centre of the square stands Pelagio Pelagi's statue of Amedeo V, **Il Conte Verde** (the Green Count), wielding his sword over two Saracen warriors.

The church of **Corpus Domini** (open daily 7.30–11.30am and 2–6pm) dates from 1603, and was erected in memory of the Miracle of Turin. The story goes that in the 15th century a French soldier brought to the city a consecrated host and chalice he had stolen en route. At the spot where the church now stands, the host miraculously flew out of the thief's pocket and stayed suspensed in midair until the bishop of Turin ordered it to come back to earth. The vault and altarpiece of the church depict the miracle (the chalice is in the Duomo and is used to celebrate Mass on Maundy Thursday). The church includes the work of Juvarra, Bernardo Vittone, and Benedetto Alfieri, who designed the black and red marble interior.

A narrow street leads to the Piazzetta Corpus Domini where Corrado Levi's *Piercing*, on the outside of the top floor of an 18th-century building, commands your attention. This late 20th-century example of urban art is a steel ring protruding from the building with red and blue paint, representing blood, and was the work of Cliostraadt – a group of young artists under the tutorship of Levi.

Via Garibaldi

Stretching from the north-west side of Piazza Castello to Piazza Statuto, **Via Garibaldi**, once the *decumanus* or main east–west axis of Roman Turin, is pedestrianised for most of its length. Lined with shops, bars and cafés, it is crowded with shoppers and office workers.

As you make your way down it, you may decide to wander into some of the pretty side streets and squares that make up the Quadrilatero Romano. This area, between Via Sant' Agostino and Via delle Orfane, is alive with restaurants offering regional, ethnic and international cuisine, literary cafés, tapas bars, wine bars and Moroccan cafés, such as **Hafa Café**, Via Sant'Agostino 23c, a little corner of Morocco redolent of the scent of mint and cinnamon. The adjoining shop sells traditional Moroccan lanterns and all kinds of exotica.

Via Garibaldi has some of the city's oldest churches, such as **Santissima Trinità** (corner of Via Garibaldi and Via XX Settembre; open Tues, Wed and Fri noon–5pm; Sat 8am–

5pm; Sun 9.30am–12.30pm and 5.30–7.30pm). Built between 1598 and 1606 to designs by ducal architect and military engineer Ascanio Vitozzi, it has some beautiful frescoes in the dome. The church is Vitozzi's last resting place.

Going west along Via Garibaldi there are several splendid baroque churches, including the **Santissimi Martiri** (Via Garibaldi 25; open daily 8am–noon and 4.30–7pm). Built by the Jesuits in 1577, this huge church is dedicated to Turin's first patron saints, martyrs Solutor, Adventor and Octavius. The vast white façade and Juvarra's high altar are unmistakeably baroque, while the nave is sumptuously adorned with bronze, marble and stucco.

North-west, parallel to Via Garibaldi at Via Carmine 3, is the church of **Madonna del Carmine** (open Mon–Sat 7.30–11.30am and 3.30–7.15pm; Sun 9am–12.30pm). Designed for the Carmelites in 1732, it was Filippo Juvarra's last

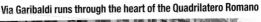

Via Garibaldi runs through the heart of the Quadrilatero Romano

work before his death in 1736. Though consecrated in that year, the church was not completed until 1870. In the apse, look for the beautiful *Madonna del Carmine*, painted by Claudio Francesco Beaumont in 1760.

Just to the north, in the church of the Confraternita del Santo Sudario, is the **Museo della Santa Sindone** (Holy Shroud Museum, Via San Domenico 28; tel: 011-436 5832; open daily 9am–noon and 3–7pm; admission fee). The museum examines the history of the Shroud and reveals the conclusions of scientific tests carried out on the cloth. The Shroud is kept under lock and key at the Duomo *(see page 29)*, but the museum has a copy.

Via Garibaldi ends at **Piazza Statuto**, the supposed heart of black magic in Turin *(see below)*. The piazza is also often

---

Black and White Magic

Turin is said to be a world centre of magic, of both the black (evil) and white (good) kinds. Occultists say it is one of the three points of the triangle of white magic (with Prague and Lyon) and the triangle of black magic (with London and San Francisco).

These beliefs go back to the time of Augustus Taurinorum, the settlement founded by the Romans at the confluence of the rivers Po and Dora. They believed that the Po represented the sun (male), and the Dora represented the moon (female), making this an ideal place for a settlement in occult terms. The laws of magic required a city to have four gates facing the four cardinal directions, and these were duly built.

The 'black heart' of the city, Piazza Statuto, was located to the west and thus, according to the Romans, in an unfavourable position as it was the site of the setting sun, the boundary between good and evil. They used the place for executions and burials; gallows stood in the piazza until the 19th century. Turin's 'white heart' is located between Piazza Reale and the royal gardens, near the Duomo and the Holy Shroud.

The best way to get around the city is by bus or tram

known as *piazza degli inglesi* since a British company known as the Italian Building Society went bankrupt before completing the square, which was originally intended to be surrounded by porticoes. The piazza is currently a building site while construction work on the metro is underway.

CITTADELLA

The Cittadella, south of the Quadrilatero Romano, centres around the remains of the Mastio della Cittadella, a 16th-century fortress. Home to the high-tech Atrium pavilion, the gallery of modern art in its 1950s building, and a museum of contemporary art in a formerly run-down neighbourhood, this area has a character very different from that of the baroque centre.

At the corner of Corso Galileo Ferraris and Via Cernaia is the former citadel's main gate – all that remains of the original building. The gate houses the oldest museum in Turin, the **Museo Storico Nazionale dell'Artiglieria e Cittadella** (National Artillery Museum; Corso Galileo Ferraris; tel: 011-562 9223; open only for temporary exhibitions). Duke Emanuele Filiberto commissioned the pentagonal citadel between 1564 and 1566, to defend Turin from French attack. It was capable of housing 3,000 soldiers and withstood three sieges, the last being in 1799. It fell ultimately to city planners in 1856, when it was deemed to be an eyesore and a deterrent to the city's spread westwards. Charting five centuries of military history, the museum was set up in 1731 by Carlo Emanuele III to educate young artillerymen and was transferred to the Mastio della Cittadella in 1893.

In front of the museum stands a statue of Pietro Micca, hero of the siege of 1706. To find out more about him, go west on the Via Cernaia towards Porta Susa station, and turn left into Via Guicciardini to the **Museo Civico Pietro Micca** (Via Gucciardini 7/a; open Sat and Sun for guided visits only; admission fee; tel: 011-546 317). Micca, a 29-year-old miner, is credited with saving Turin from French invaders on the night of 29 August 1706. The city had been under siege for four months and on that night French forces had infiltrated the tunnels beneath the citadel. By lighting a fuse, Micca succeeded in collapsing part of a tunnel, so blocking the intruders and protecting the city. But it cost Micca and his fellow miners their lives. Subsequent theories have suggested less heroic explanations for Micca's act: that his fuse was too short, that he had been acting against his will, that he simply wasn't capable of running fast enough to escape the explosion. Whatever the explanation, the fact remains that Turin was saved from certain defeat by his actions, and Micca became a symbol of Italian resistance to foreign domination.

The highlight of the museum is the network of tunnels beneath the Cittadella. Torchlit tours take place every 35 minutes 9.35am–12.05pm and every hour 1.20–6.20pm (tel: 011-

546 317; closed in winter until the end of April).

Atrium Torino

Just over to the east, the Via Pietro Micca comes to an end at Piazza Solferino, which is now the site of Turin's splendidly futuristic twin buildings, called **Atrium Torino** (open daily 9.30am–7pm; guided tours by reservation, tel: 011-517 8134). Two enormous pavilions, crafted in wood, steel and glass in the shape of a prism, or, as some say, the *gianduiotto* chocolate, snake their way through a leafy thoroughfare. Designer Giorgetto Giugiaro,

Atrium Torino

best known for his many car designs for Maserati and Alfa Romeo Visconti, was the architect. Each building houses a large exhibition space over two floors.

Both pavilions are run by the city council. One of them, **AtriumCittà**, explains the current transformation of Turin, including the multi-million euro Rail Bypass (Passante Ferroviario) project, which involves the concealing of 12km (7½ miles) of railway line underground, a project due for completion in 2012. Construction of the new Metro is also detailed. The other pavilion, **Atrium2006**, is given over to the Winter Olympics, charting the history of snow sports and detailing the events of 2006. The city's main tourist information office is also here, and you can hire bicycles for free.

Modern Art in Turin

Turin may be a baroque treasure house, but the city also has excellent collections of the art of our own times. For a taste of this side of Turin, head south, beyond the Piazza Vittorio Emanuele II and its statue of the ruler aloft a tall pedestal, to the GAM or **Galleria Civica d'Arte Moderna e Contemporanea**, (Via Magenta 31; tel: 011-562 9911: open Tues–Sun 9am–7pm; admission fee). The long, grey 1950s building houses one of the country's most important collections of modern and contemporary art, with the emphasis on Italian works.

> The 'impoverished art' movement originated from the Impoverished Theatre of Polish playwright, Jerzy Grotowsky. A group of artists showcased natural or worthless materials at the GAM in 1967. The sculptures included various primitive forms of human habitation, such as giant igloos covered in canvas.

A generous selection of the gallery's 15,000 works of art is on show. The first floor is devoted to the 20th century and includes a considerable number of significant works by the avant-garde Arte Povera (impoverished art) movement of the 1960s. On the second floor you can see pieces by well-known international figures such as Paul Klee, Amedeo Modigliani and Max Ernst, alongside Italian artists such as Massimo D'Azeglio, Fontanesi, Pelizza da Volpedo and Felice Casorati. The gallery has a particularly strong collection of video art.

If the GAM is modern, the **Fondazione Sandretto Re Rebaudengo** is positively futuristic (Via Modane 16; tel: 011-1983 1600; open Tues–Sun noon–8pm and Thur until 11pm; admission fee). Set in the rather run-down San Paolo neighbourhood south of the Corso Vittorio Emanuele II, this huge, minimalist exhibition space was designed by the architect Claudio Silvestrin and opened in 2002. Inside, all forms of contemporary art are on display – painting, sculpture, photography, video, installations, performances – from a wide variety of practitioners. Those experiencing gallery fatigue or in need of sustenance might like to try the foundation's very pleasant café – the Spazio Caffeteria – or the restaurant on the first floor.

Nearby, to the south, the so-called **Spina** runs from Largo Orbassano to Caselle airport in the north. This 'Spine' or 'backbone' follows the route of Turin's railway, which is being sunk below ground level. When construction is finished, this former eyesore will look completely different: a tree-lined road and cycle track, together with islands of contemporary sculpture. Of the 11 artistic installations planned, two are on display, Giuseppe Pennone's *Giardino di Cefalonia a Corfu* and Mario Merz's *Igloo*.

Contemporary art in a minimalist setting at the Fondazione

CENTRO CITTÀ

Via Po and Via Roma are lined with colonnaded walkways

The grid of streets between Via Po and Via Roma are, for the Torinesi, the centre of town. The heart and symbol of this area is the elegant, arcaded Via Roma, Turin's principal thoroughfare, lined with the most exclusive shops and designer names. Also here is the Piazza Carignano, the city's political centre in the 19th century. Its palazzo, the seat of Italy's first parliament from 1861 to 1864, today houses the museum of the Risorgimento. Opposite is the historic Teatro Carignano, and nearby are some of the city's most important museums, including the Egyptian Museum, and the Galleria Sabauda, with its extensive Savoy art collection. Piazza San Carlo is home to beautiful baroque palaces, churches, elegant historic cafés and prestigious clothes shops. Other activities on offer include a walk in Valentino Park, a promenade along the riverside and a boat trip on the Po.

Via Roma

The **Via Roma** is Turin's main street, elegantly colonnaded and bristling with cafés and chic shops. The road follows the course of two sets of Roman walls, flattened in the 1620s to make a long, straight avenue, which was originally called Via Nuova. This 17th-century section leads south from Piazza Castello, whose colonnaded walkways provide shelter from rain and summer sun. Elegant shops and designer boutiques grace these portals, from the modestly priced Upim department store at No. 305 to the ritzy Hermès at No. 124.

Around Via Roma

Just to the south-east of the first section of the Via Roma, the Via Accademia delle Scienze leads down to the **Piazza Carignano**. The baroque **Palazzo Carignano** (Via Accademia delle Scienze 5) is a superb example of Guarino Guarini's design, with a splendid curved red-brick façade and ornate rotunda. It was built between 1679 and 1684 for Prince Emanuele Filiberto Carignano and later was the birthplace of Carlo Alberto and of Vittorio Emanuele II, who went on to become the first king of Italy.

After the unification of Italy in 1861, this former royal residence was used as the first national parliament building. The

Palazzo Carignano held Italy's first parliament from 1861–4

restored ballroom-amphitheatre – resplendent in red velvet like a small, plush theatre – was once the parliamentary chamber. The palazzo now houses the **Museo Nazionale del Risorgimento Italiano** (open Tues–Sun 9am–7pm; admission fee; tel: 011-562 1147), which explains how the various Italian states came together to create one nation. Artefacts, paintings and a documentary in English tell the story of the movement and its key players – Count Cavour, Giuseppe Garibaldi and Giuseppe Mazzini.

Opposite the museum is **Ristorante Il Cambio**, Cavour's favourite restaurant, and the sumptuously decorated **Teatro Carignano**, built originally in 1711, then rebuilt to a design by Benedetto Alfieri. It has subsequently burnt down twice, and the present building is the work of 18th-century Giovanni Battista Feroggio.

Egyptian Museum

On the south side of the square, in Guarini's Palazzo dell'Accademia delle Scienze, is the **Museo Egizio** (Via Accademia delle Scienze 6; tel: 011-561 7776; open Tues–Sun 8.30am–7.30pm; admission fee – option to buy a joint ticket allowing entry to the Galleria Sabauda). Quite simply, the Egyptian Museum of Turin is the most important museum of Egyptology in the world after the one in Cairo. The collection has its origins in the 17th century, but it grew massively in the early 19th century after Carlo Felice became interested in Egyptian culture in the wake of Napoleon's campaigns in that country. He acquired a substantial number of the finds collected by the Piedmontese Bernardino Drovetti, stationed in Egypt as French Consul General during the Napoleonic Wars. Finds from digs by the Italian Archeological Mission entered the collection in the early 20th century, and new pieces were also added between 1930 and 1969. Today, the museum has about 30,000 pieces.

The ground floor's first room displays sculptures, reconstructed temples and household objects dated between 6,000 and 3,500BC. Also on this floor is a copy of the **Rosetta Stone**. The inscriptions on the original, found in Egypt in 1799 and now in the British Museum, gave experts the key to deciphering hieroglyphs, which had previously been unreadable. Also here are the 'Palermo stone', inscribed with a list of sovereigns from the mythical age to the Fifth Dynasty, and the 'Royal Canon papyrus', listing the sequence of Egyptian sovereigns in succession. The museum's collection of papyri is often considered to be the most important set of Egyptian written documents in the world.

Part of the Egyptian Museum's collection of statuary

In the **underground section**, a large part of the city's Roman walls can be seen, 2.5m (8ft) thick and 7m (23ft) high, unearthed during renovation. This area is devoted to the Excavations of the Italian Archeological Mission in Asyut, Qau el Kebir and Gebelein. A flight of steps leads up to the reconstructed Temple of Ellesiya, which dates from around 1430BC. The temple was donated by the Egyptian government in the 1960s in recognition of Italy's help in saving monuments destined to be submerged by the Aswan Dam Project. More monuments can be seen in the nearby Statuary Rooms, including a highlight of the museum: a black granite statue of the 13th-century BC ruler Ramses II.

The first floor of the museum is crammed full of sarcophagi and mummies. Lengthy restoration of the upper floors is underway, and at present many rooms are closed. However, one of the star sights is still on display – the tomb of Kha and Merit, which dates from about 1430BC. Discovered in 1906 by Italian archeologists in Deir el Medina, it houses sarcophagi and statues, as well as furniture, garments, grooming items, vases of unguents and preserved food – all deemed to be necessities for the afterlife of Kha and his bride.

Housed in the same building as the Egyptian Museum is the **Galleria Sabauda** (Via Accademia delle Scienze 6; tel: 011-547 440; open Tues, Fri, Sat and Sun 8.30am–2pm; Wed 2–7.30pm; Thur 10am–7.30pm; admission fee). The gallery, made up of the main art collection of the house of Savoy, is one of the country's richest treasure troves of paintings from the 14th to 18th centuries. Among the highlights in the Italian Masters section are works by Veronese, Bellini and Mantegna, and a section by Piedmontese artists, including Gaudenzio Ferrari and Defendente Ferrari. Flemish and Dutch artists, such as Jan Van Eyck and Van Dyck, are well represented, as are French works, including landscape paintings by Poussin and Claude Lorrain. The collection is scheduled to move to the Palazzo Reale's Manica Nuova in 2007.

> **Those with a serious sweet tooth will find their version of paradise on the eastern side of the Piazza San Carlo at No. 191 in Confetteria Stratta (open Tues–Sat 9.30am–7.30pm, Mon 3–7.30pm). Established in 1836, it has all kinds of tempting chocolates and sweets from *gianduiotti* to *marrons glacés*.**

An iconic sign in the colonnaded walkways of Piazza San Carlo

Opposite the Galleria Sabauda, in Via Maria Vittoria, is Turin's largest church, **San Filippo Neri** (open Mon–Sat 8am–noon and 5.30–7pm; Sun 10am–noon). Its origins can be traced back to the second half of the 17th century, but Juvarra played a large part in its design, and its later neoclassical façade was added by Carlo Giuseppe Talucchi. The single nave is 31m (102ft) high, but, perhaps surprisingly, the church has superb acoustics and is the splendid setting for many concerts, especially during the classical music festival, Settembre Musica *(see page 94)*.

Piazza San Carlo

Turning west back onto the Via Roma, the 17th-century section of this lovely street ends at the baroque **Piazza San Carlo**, known as *il salotto di Torino* (Turin's salon, or drawing room). Lined by designer shops and cafés, San Carlo is one of Europe's largest public squares. Major construction work has taken place in the piazza to make it entirely pedestrianised, with underground car parking, in time for the Winter Olympics.

A 19th-century equestrian monument to Duke Emanuele Filiberto decorates the middle of the piazza. On the south side are twin 17th-century churches, San Carlo Borromeo and Santa Cristina. **San Carlo Borromeo** (open Mon–Fri 7.10am–noon and 4–6.30pm; Sat and Sun 9am–noon and 4–6.30pm) was begun in the 17th century, but the façade dates from 1834, inspired by Juvarra's design for the twin church of Santa Cristina. The relief on the façade shows San Carlo Borromeo, the 16th-century bishop of Milan, giving thanks for the cessation of the plague, and pledging to walk to Chambéry, then home of the Holy Shroud. A Bernardino Quadri painting over the high altar depicts the veneration of the Shroud by San Carlo.

Enjoy a restorative drink in regal surroundings at Caffè Torino

Situated just opposite is the church of **Santa Cristina** (open daily 8.30am–12.30pm and 4–7pm), designed in 1653 by Carlo di Castellamonte and commissioned by Marie Christine of France (Madama Reale). The ubiquitous Juvarra added the façade in 1715–18.

Also on the Piazza San Carlo are two of Turin's most famous and historic cafés. The **Caffè San Carlo** (Piazza San Carlo 156; open Tues–Sun 8am–midnight, Fri and Sat until 1am; closed Mon) was the first Italian café to be lit by gas, in 1832. The regal atmosphere is embellished with stucco and statues, the food is of superior quality and the coffee is excellent. **Caffè Torino** (Piazza San Carlo 204; open daily 7.30am–1am) is just as prestigious as its neighbour, although its elegant interiors date to the early 20th century. Its specialities are patisseries and delicious *giandujoni* (large hazelnut chocolates).

Just to the west of the piazza is the Church of Santa Teresa, home to the **Museo della Marionetta** (Via Santa Teresa 5; tel: 011-530 238; open by appointment only; admission fee). This valuable collection of thousands of period hand and string puppets was put together by the Lupi family, puppeteers who arrived in Turin in the early 1800s. The oldest piece is an 18th-century Harlequin (Arlecchino). There are many representations of Turin's character, Gianduja, from the Commedia dell'arte theatre tradition; with his three-pointed hat, enormous red nose and pigeon chest, Gianduja is instantly recognisable.

> You will always be assured of drinking good coffee in Turin, home of Lavazza coffee. Café society flourishes in this city. Whether it's a regal, chandeliered, historic establishment, such as Caffè San Carlo, a famous hang-out of Nietzsche, such as Caffè Elena, or the little piece of Morocco that is the Hafa Café, you really are spoilt for choice.

Continuing south from the Piazza San Carlo, the Via Roma takes on a different persona. It still has all-weather porticoes and is still as imposing as its more northerly reaches, but this section is a product of the ordered, grandiose design of Marcello Piacentini, Mussolini's favourite architect. Past the statues of figures representing the city's two major rivers, the Po and Dora, the Via Roma finally ends at the Piazza San Carlo, overlooked by the **Porta Nuova railway station**, the city's main terminus for international and national rail services. When built, between 1861 and 1868, it was the latest thing in railway architecture, using iron and glass. Its role as rail hub is due to be taken over by Porta Susa station, near Piazza Statuto, in the next few years.

Turin's dreaming spire

Around Via Po

From the Piazza Castello, the Via Po runs at right angles to the Via Roma down to the River Po. Just like its sister street, the Via Po's porticoes afford shelter from the rain and shady respite from the heat.

In the early 19th century, Vittorio Emanuele I used the Via Po as his favourite perambulation from his palace down to the river. One reminder of the royal past is the **Caffè Fiorio**, at No. 8 (open Tues–Thur and Sun 8am–1am; Fri and Sat 8am–2am), which first opened its doors in 1780. Amid the marble and plush red décor, those with power and influence in the kingdom, notably Count Cavour, once met here to plan their next move. Power politics aside, among the main draws today is the *gianduja gelato* (chocolate hazelnut ice cream).

Turin's **Università** (university), built in 1714, is close by at Via Po 15. The

> The symbol of the house of Savoy – a winged being with the palm of victory in his left hand and spear in the right, and a star over his head – was used to decorate the pinnacle of the spire of the Mole. After it was struck by lightning in 1954, it was replaced by a star. The Savoy symbol is now displayed inside the Museum of Cinema.

wrought-iron gate is by Filippo Juvarra and, although you cannot enter, you can peek past the double loggia of pillars into the lovely courtyard.

Mole Antonelliana

To the east of the university, looming above the rooftops, is an unmissable sight, the **Mole Antonelliana** (Via Montebello 20; tel: 011-812 5658). Capped by a spire reaching 167m (530ft) high, it was designed by architect Alessandro Antonelli at the end of the 19th century as a synagogue. Occupying a small piece of land, its planned height was due to be just 47m (154ft). However, Antonelli decided that the only way was upwards, his plans becoming steadily more ambitious, until the Jewish elders, alarmed at the financial implications of such a project, finally washed their hands of it.

This spectacular white elephant became a memorial to Vittorio Emanuele II and later housed the Risorgimento museum before falling into neglect. Since 2000, its star quality has been assured as the home of the excellent **Museo Nazionale del Cinema** (National Museum of Cinema; open

Tues–Sun 10am–8pm; Sat 10am–11pm; admission fee). The Italian film industry was born in Turin, which from 1906 to 1916 was the world film production capital until overtaken by Hollywood (and, in Italy, by Rome). Spread over five levels of the building, the museum outlines the story of the cinema, using everything from classic clips, such as the shower scene from *Psycho* and the car chase in *The Italian Job*; through props like the egg from *Alien* and the head from *Jaws*; and on to costumes, ranging from Marilyn Monroe's bodice and Charlie Chaplin's bowler hat to Fellini's scarf, coat and hat. One section is dedicated to the 'pre-history' of cinema – shadow theatres, optical boxes, magic lanterns, 19th-century equipment, chronophotographs – and culminates in the Lumière Brothers' historic début of their cinematograph system at the Grand Café de Paris in 1895.

The Cinema Museum's inner sanctum

At the heart of the museum is the Aula del Tempio (temple room), equipped with comfortable loungers in which you can enjoy clips from films of today and yesterday on giant screens. Ten themed 'chapels' are arranged around this main hall, dedicated to cult films – from horror, sci-fi, love and death to animation, the absurd and experimental cinema. Sequences from 200 films are screened. In the Macchina del Cinema (Cinema Machine) section, the craft of film-making is revealed – editing, sound effects, casting and much more. The museum's stylish **Ciak Bar** serves snacks and *aperitivi*, as well as more substantial meals.

A visit to the Mole Antonelliana should include a ride in the panoramic, glass-walled lift which, in less than a minute, soars up to a viewing platform 85m (279ft) up on the spire of the building (lift open Tues–Fri 10am–8pm; Sat 10am–11pm; Sun 10am–8pm; ticket office closes one hour earlier; admission fee). The views over the city and towards the Alps are wonderful.

Towards Piazza Vittorio Veneto

Returning to the colonnaded Via Po, go past the stalls loaded with second-hand books, for which this street is a mecca, and you will come to the **Museo di Arti Decorative – Fondazione Pietro Accorsi** (Museum of Decorative Arts; Via Po 55; tel: 011-8129 116; open Tues–Sun 10am–8pm, Thur until 11pm; admission fee). Housed in the elegant 18th-century house of Pietro Accorsi, a Piedmontese antiques dealer, this museum opened in 1999. Thousands of pieces of furniture, porcelain, silver, paintings, tapestries and objets d'art – many from the 18th century – make up the collection. The museum also stages temporary exhibitions, art history classes and concerts.

Off the south side of the Via Po is the **Pinacoteca dell' Accademia Albertina di Belle Arti** (Via Accademia Albertina 8; tel: 011-817 7862; open Tues–Sun 9am–1pm and 3–7pm; admission fee). The highlights of the academy are the works of Caravaggesque and Flemish painters from the 15th to 18th centuries. Look also for the splendid 16th-century collection of 60 *cartoni* (cartoons) by the local artist Gaudenzio Ferrari.

Not far south from the academy is the **Piazza Carlo Emanuele II**, known as **Piazza Carlina**, perhaps as an ill-veiled reference to Carlo Emanuele's gay leanings. At the centre of this pretty, French-style piazza is a neoclassical statue of Cavour, by Sienese sculptor Giovanni Dupré.

The Via Po ends in the lovely **Piazza Vittorio Veneto**, locally known as simply **Piazza Vittorio**, overlooking the river and the green hill beyond, La Collina *(see page 56)*. Wine bars and cafés line this monumental square, which bristles with porticoes and palazzi. Although at first glance the piazza appears to be baroque, it was as late as 1825 that the architect Giuseppe Frizzi put his neoclassical design into effect.

Parco del Valentino

The Murazzi embankment runs along the river. Following it upstream is a pleasant way to reach the **Parco del Valentino**, the city's largest park, covering approximately 55 hectares (135 acres). By day it is the people's park, full of walkers, rollerbladers, cyclists, joggers, picnickers, lovers and those who just want to relax by the banks of the river away from the bustle of the city; by night it buzzes with clubs and bars.

In the middle of the park, the impressive 16th-century Castello del Valentino (closed to the public), once a royal residence of the Savoys, is today the University of Turin's Faculty of Architecture. Just to the

Two boats, the *Valentino* and *Valentina*, ply the River Po and can be boarded at Murazzi at the end of Piazza Vittorio Veneto or from Borgo Medioevale. For information tel: 011-5764 733, for bookings tel: 011-744 892. Boats run Tues–Sun, from early June to late September; at other times service is restricted to Sundays and holidays.

Piazza Vittorio Veneto viewed from the Po

north of it is a small botanical garden, **Orto Botanico** (Viale P.A. Mattioli; tel: 011-661 2447; open Sat, Sun and holidays 9am–1pm and 3–7pm; admission fee). The garden, which has centuries-old trees and a herbarium with around 700,000 specimens, specialises in the cultivation of medicinal and alpine plants, including rare species.

Walking south through the park from here, you eventually come to the **Borgo e Rocca Medioevale** (Medieval Village and Fort; Viale Virgilio, Parco del Valentino; Borgo open Mon–Sun 9am–7pm, free; Rocca open Tues–Sun 9am–7pm, admission fee). This reconstruction of a 15th-century village and castle was created for the General Italian Exhibition of 1884, a time when all things medieval were in fashion. The builders went to great lengths to be as faithful as possible to the period, basing their designs on particular medieval Piedmontese structures to try to bring a sense of verisimilitude to the project.

LA COLLINA

From Piazza Vittorio there are splendid views across the river to the green hill known as **La Collina** on the right bank. Backed by the natural amphitheatre of hill and snow-capped peaks in the distance, this beautiful area is the most exclusive residential site in Turin, full of Liberty-style villas gazing down over the city centre. It is also the site of two landmark churches, a museum of mountain culture and a glorious baroque basilica perched on the hill. The often steep slopes make this a good place for long walks.

Cross the river on the Ponte Vittorio Emanuele I. Just ahead of you are the classical columns and imposing dome crowning the church of **Gran Madre di Dio** (open Mon–Sat 7.30am–noon and 4.30–7pm, Sun also 8.30–10pm). Modelled on Rome's ancient Pantheon, this church, dedi-

The church of Gran Madre di Dio

cated to the 'great mother of God', was built to celebrate Vittorio Emanuele I's return from exile after the Napoleonic Wars, and is now a symbol of the city of Turin. Designed by Ferdinando Bonsignore between 1827 and 1831, it is laid out in the symmetrical neoclassical style on a central plan. Its grandiose staircase became famous as one of the

Young Torinesi

locations used in the original version of the film *The Italian Job*. It is also well known among aficionados of white magic as being the location of the Holy Grail, which is reputed to be hidden under or near the church.

A steepish climb of about 15 minutes from Gran Madre church leads up to the Monte dei Cappuccini and the church of **Santa Maria del Monte** (Via Giardino 35; open daily 9am–noon and 3–7.30pm), at a height of over 240m (800ft) above sea level. The views over the city from here are truly memorable. Built in 1584 to a design by the architect Ascanio Vitozzi, the church adjoins a still-working Capuchin convent.

Turin has always had a close connection with the nearby Alps. The story of this relationship unfolds at the **Museo Nazionale della Montagna 'Duca degli Abruzzi'** (National Mountain Museum; Via Giardino 39; tel: 011-660 4104; due to reopen late 2005), located next to the church and convent. Named after Luigi di Savoia, Duke of Abruzzi (1873–1942), who was a passionate mountaineer, the museum diplays many artefacts collected during his expeditions, as well as information on the natural alpine environment and the history of mountaineering and skiing. But the highlight for many can be found on the top floor; here the **Vedetta Alpina** – literally a window on the Alps – gives majestic views that range all the way from Monte Rosa (on the Swiss border) to Monviso (on the French border).

Villa della Regina

South of here a long road leads up to the **Villa della Regina** (Strada Santa Margherita 40; tel: 011-819 5035). Terraced parkland surrounds this beautiful palace, which was once the hillside residence of Queen Anne d'Orléans. Its design has Filippo Juvarra's unmistakeable signature imprinted upon it and this, coupled with its breathtaking views over the city, have made this place a UNESCO World Heritage Site. Although closed for restoration at the moment, when it re-opens the palace will serve partly as a museum and partly as an archive documenting restoration work in Piedmont.

Basilica di Superga

East of the centre of Turin, at a height of 660m (2,160ft), stands Juvarra's beautiful **Basilica di Superga** (Strada della Basilica di Superga 73; open daily 9am–12.45pm and 3–6.45pm, until 5.45pm Nov–March; admission fee). The best way to get here is by the funicular, 'La Cremagliera', which runs from Sassi station (accessible from the city on tram 15 or buses 61 and 68) through glorious countryside and with panoramic views over the Monferrato hills.

In 1706, during the French siege of Turin, Vittorio Amedeo II prayed on this site, pledging to build a basilica here if the Virgin Mary protected the city. Filippo Juvarra set to work 10 years later using stones *(sassi)* taken from the bottom of the hill, an area ever since known as Sassi and the departure point of the funicular railway. The basilica was inaugurated by Carlo Emanuele II in 1731. It is 54m (177ft) long, 34m (111ft)

High on a hill, the Basilica di Superga

wide, and the magnificent dome, reminiscent of St Paul's in London, rises 65m (213ft) high. In the left transept, the Cappella del Voto (chapel) contains the wooden statue of the Madonna commemorating the spot where Vittorio Amedeo made his vow to Mary during the siege of Turin. The crypt houses a grandiose mausoleum containing the Savoy tombs, including rulers from Vittorio Amedeo II to Carlo Alberto, and 50 other princely members of the family.

On 4 May 1949 a plane carrying the Grande Torino football team from a match in Lisbon crashed into the hillside, killing everyone on board. A large stone plaque outside the basilica commemorating the tragedy is an object of pilgrimage for local fans. Located off the cloister of the basilica, the **Museo del Grande Torino** (open daily Apr–Oct 4.30–7.30pm; Nov–Mar until 6.30pm) has the team's memorabilia on display and reminders of their prowess as Italian football league champions for five consecutive years.

Lingotto's test track was a setting for crime caper *The Italian Job*

LINGOTTO

The area south of the city centre was the heart of Turin's car industry. It was the Fiat company (Fabbrica Italiana Automobili Torino), founded in 1899, that made Turin *the* city of cars. The areas of Lingotto, Italia 61, Mirafiori and Millefonti, once the powerhouse of the industry, are now being spruced up in a multi-million euro 'suburbs project', with many new sporting facilities constructed for the 2006 Winter Olympic Games.

A reminder of the importance of the motor car to Turin is the **Museo dell'Automobile 'Carlo Biscaretti di Ruffia'** (Car Museum; Corso Unità d'Italia 40; tel: 011-677 666; open Tues–Sat 10am–6.30pm; Thur until 10pm; Sun 10am–8.30pm; admission fee). The museum is located on the banks of the River Po in what was once a splendid example of modern architecture, designed in the late 1950s by Amedeo Albertini, although it is now in dire need of care. Its collection of vehicles, one of Europe's best, charts the evolution of the motor vehicle, from the car's forerunners of the second half of the 18th century through the 'horseless carriages' of the late 19th century and on to the latest models. Everything from sleek racing Ferraris and Alfa Romeos to the 500 Topolino – Fiat's first popularised model from the 1930s – is on display over the museum's three floors.

Nearby, between the Corso Unità d'Italia and Via Ventimiglia, is the area known as **Italia 61**, built in 1961 to celebrate the centenary of the unification of Italy. One of the original buildings has been redesigned and rechristened the **Palavela** (Via Ventimiglia), a 9,000-seat Olympic venue for ice figure skating. The eye-catching 1961 sail-shaped roof designed by Annibale and Giorgio Rigotti remains.

South of here is the concrete **Palazzo del Lavoro** (Via Ventimiglia 201), designed by Pier Luigi Nervi in the late 1950s. Large enough to contain St Peter's in Rome, this enormous structure, propped up by concrete columns and metal 'umbrellas', stages trade fairs and exhibitions.

Just west of Italia 61 is **Lingotto**, the cultural and trade centre which has risen on the site of the old Fiat factory. Construction began in 1917 on what was the largest car factory in Europe, occupying five floors and with a parabolic test track on the roof. The factory became Europe's blueprint for the efficient mass production of motor cars. By 1939, the huge Mirafiori

Lingotto's southern ramp leads up to the rooftop test track

Fiat factory to the south had overtaken it, but production continued at Lingotto until 1982. Transformation came under the skilful eye of architect Renzo Piano starting in 1986, when it became a multi-purpose exhibition centre which today is the setting for events such as the Salone del Gusto, the biannual international fair of the Slow Food movement *(see page 72)*. Apart from exhibition space, Lingotto encompasses an auditorium, a large shopping mall and two hotels, the Meridien and Art+Tech. The latter is Turin's only five-star hotel. Hotel guests can use the former Fiat test track for jogging. From the roof there are stunning views over the city and across to the Alps.

Renzo Piano managed to find room on the Lingotto rooftop for two striking-looking buildings. The first is the **Pinacoteca Giovanni e Marella Agnelli** (open Tues–Sun 9am–7pm; admission fee; tel: 011-006 2713), known as the *scrigno* (jewel case). Made of wood, it has a glass roof in order to give natural light to the selection of treasures from the art collection of the Agnelli family, the owners of Fiat. Twenty-five pieces are on display, including seven works by Matisse, six by Canaletto, two Picassos, dancers sculpted by Antonio Canova, a Renoir, Manet's *La Négresse* and Modigliani's famous *Nue Couchée*.

Piano's other design is La Bolla (the bubble), a bubble-shaped glass-and-steel rooftop meeting room for exhibition delegates. Unfortunately, it is not open to the public.

ROYAL RESIDENCES

The circle of palaces and castles around the city, built by the house of Savoy between the 17th and 19th centuries, came to be known as the *corona di delizi*, or crown of delights. In 1997 UNESCO added this crown to the register of World Heritage Sites (for opening times and visiting details, *see page 64*).

To the West

West of the city at the entrance to the Valle di Susa lies the **Castello di Rivoli**. This imposing baroque building was part of a grand design begun by Filippo Juvarra in 1718 at the behest of Vittorio Amedeo II. Since 1984, these antique surroundings have been home to some rather more modern artworks. The castle houses Turin's **Museo d'Arte Contemporanea**, which includes the works of Gilbert and George, Jeff Koons and Maurizio Cattelan.

The Manica Lunga (long sleeve) gallery was originally built in the mid-17th century to house the painting collection of Carlo Emanuele I, and now, since restoration was completed in 1998, it is the new wing of the museum. Access to the castle's floors is by a new hanging staircase supported by steel tie beams, designed by Andrea Bruno, the architect responsible for the restoration of the entire building. Along

The Castello di Rivoli is home to Turin's Contemporary Art Museum

with around 400 works in the permanent collection, which are exhibited on a rotating basis, major temporary exhibitions are also staged. There is also a good museum café and restaurant.

To the South

Located in the southern suburbs of Turin, **Palazzina di Caccia di Stupinigi** was the favourite hunting lodge of the Savoys and was once surrounded by a huge forest. Approached along a straight, tree-lined avenue, the palace is

---

Visiting the Royal Residences

Castello di Rivoli Piazza Mafalda di Savoia; tel: 011-956 5222; open Tues–Thur 10am–5pm and Fri–Sun 10am–9pm; admission fee; shuttle bus from Piazza Castello Sat 2.45pm and 5pm, Sun and public holidays 10.15am, noon, 3pm and 4.30pm.

Palazzina di Caccia di Stupinigi Piazza Principe Amedeo 7; tel: 011-358 1220; open Apr–Oct Tues–Sun 10am–6pm; Nov–Mar until 5pm; last entry 1 hour earlier; admission fee; bus 36 from Piazza Castello.

Castello di Moncalieri Piazza Baden Baden 4, Moncalieri; tel: 011-640 2833; open Thur, Sat and Sun 8.30am–6.30pm; admission fee; buses from Turin include 35, 40, 45 and 67.

Castello di Racconigi Via Morosini 1; tel: 017-284 005; open Tues–Sun 8.30am–7.30pm; admission fee; park open Mar–Nov Tues–Sun 10am until dusk; admission fee; Cuneo line train from Turin to Racconigi.

Reggia di Venaria Reale Piazza della Repubblica 4; tel: 011-459 3675; open Tues, Thur, Sat and Sun 9.30am–12.30pm and 2.30–6.30pm; admission fee. Some parts can be seen by guided tours (included in ticket price); advance reservations, tel: 011-459 3675 or 011-496 272. Buses 11 and 72 from Turin, then 800m (½ mile) on foot.

Castello Ducale di Agliè Piazza del Castello 2; tel: 0124-330102; open Tues–Sun 8.30am–7.30pm; admission fee. Park open May–Oct Tues–Sun 9am–1pm and 2–7.30pm. GTI bus from Turin, tel: 800-990 097.

instantly recognisable from a distance by the statue of a stag on top of the roof. Commissioned by Vittorio Amedeo II, the palace was designed by Filippo Juvarra in the European rococo style – which succeeded the baroque period – full of light, curves and movement. The palace houses the **Museo dell'ammobiliamento**, a furnishings museum.

Stupinigi, delight of the Savoys

The most important nucleus of furniture of the palace is the work of the great cabinet-maker Pietro Piffetti (1700–77), who, following Juvarra's ideas, created the most original and elegant forms in the rococo style (unfortunately, many of the Piffetti pieces were stolen in a burglary in 2004). The library, painted in the blue and yellow colours of Turin, leads into the Eastern apartments full of chinoiserie and now, sadly, the empty spaces where once stood the missing furniture.

In the Hall of Mirrors (Saletta degli Specchi) is Turin's first marble bath, installed at the request of Paolina Borghese, sister of Napoleon and wife of one of the French leader's generals, Camillo Borghese. The Perspectives Room was entirely painted by Giovan Battista Alberoni, and is full of trompe l'oeil motifs. The eliptical Central Hall in the King's Chambers is lit by a huge crystal chandelier, while on the walls are dozens of wall lamps appliquéd with deer heads. This ballroom is still used as a function hall. The Queen's Chambers include the best ceiling in the palace – an extraordinary work depicting *The Sacrifice of Iphigenia* – one of the masterpieces of Italian rococo painting, by Venetian Giovan Battista Crosato. The Sant'Uberto

Stupinigi's elliptical Central Hall

Chapel is full of frescoes and trompe l'oeils, as well as some rather ugly cherubs *(putti)*, painted after Juvarra's death, of which he certainly would not have approved. The 19th-century apartments are under restoration and areas of the palace are liable to be closed due to lack of staff.

On the banks of the Po, south of Turin, **Castello di Moncalieri** dates back to medieval times and was one of the favourite retreats of Italy's first king, Vittorio Emanuele II. The park was the setting for his romantic trysts with his mistress, the 'bela Rosin'. The castello is now the barracks of the *carabinieri*, and only three of its royal apartments can be visited – those belonging to the king, his wife Queen Maria Adelaide and their grand-daughter Maria Letizia.

South of Turin, an 11th-century fortress, **Castello di Racconigi**, became the Savoys' official residence under Carlo Alberto in the early 18th century. Pelagio Pelagi had a hand in its design, but its style incorporates both the baroque and the neoclassical. The lovely park was originally laid out by André Le Nôtre in the 1600s, but acquired a wilder look in the early 19th century. Within the grounds are structures that include Merlin's cave, a Swiss chalet and a Russian dacha. Bicycles are available for hire in the park and a little train does tours of the palace grounds.

To the North

North of the city, **Reggia di Venaria Reale**, the so-called Turinese Versailles, was the Savoys' hunting estate. Commissioned in the mid-17th century by Carlo Emanuele II, it was dedicated to Diana, goddess of hunting. The largest, most impressive room is the Salone di Diana (open for guided visits) at the centre of the palace. Juvarra's church of Sant'Uberto is also open, as is Michelangelo Garove's Pavilion. Restoration is in progress, to be completed in 2006. The nearby **Parco Regionale La Mandria** (Via Carlo Emanuele 11; open daily Mar–Sept 8am–8pm; Oct–Feb daily 8am–5pm; admission free) was once a stud farm and is now a nature reserve.

To the far north of the city, a large park and lovely gardens frame **Castello Ducale di Agliè**, which was once the holiday home of Carlo Felice (1821–31) and Maria Cristina of Bourbon. Before the reign of the Savoys it was the residence of the count and writer Filippo d'Agliè, and was designed by Amedeo di Castellamonte from an existing medieval castle. In the park, look for the monumental fountain designed in 1770 by the Collina brothers.

Reggia di Venaria Reale

PIEDMONT'S WINELANDS

Wedged between the Alps and the Ligurian Sea, Piedmont has a great range of landscapes and attractions, from dining opportunities to winter sports, and including palaces, fortresses, holy mounts and pretty villages.

Piedmont's main wine-producing areas, Le Langhe and Il Monferrato, lie among rolling hills and are within easy driving distance of Turin. Far more dramatic in character are the alpine regions near the Swiss and French borders.

Le Langhe

Some of Italy's finest wines come from Le Langhe, the hilly region south of Turin between the Tanaro and Bormida rivers at an altitude of 450–800m (1,500–2,600ft). This is also the home of the white truffle – the 'white gold' of Piedmont.

Grinzane Cavour's medieval castle amid Piedmont's winelands

Alba

The capital, **Alba**, is a relatively easy drive 62km (39
miles) south of Turin in the
Langa Bassa set among vine-
clad hills. Several medieval
red-brick towers rising above
the town tell of its importance during the Middle
Ages, although the Romans
were here long before. At the
heart of town is the Piazza
Risorgimento, once the site

> **Depicted on the
> Cattedrale di San
> Lorenzo's exterior wall
> are the symbols of the
> four Evangelists,
> Matthew, Mark, Luke
> and John. They give a
> clue to the origins of the
> town's name:** *Angelo*
> (angel) for Matthew,
> *Leone* (lion) for Mark,
> *Bue* (ox) for Luke and
> *Aquila* (eagle) for John.

of the Roman forum, now dominated by the red-brick **Cattedrale di San Lorenzo** (under restoration but normally open
daily 7am–noon and 3–6.30pm). This has been the site of a
church since the 7th century, but the overall impression nowadays is more Lombard Gothic. Among the most interesting
details are the bell tower, the wooden choir from the 16th century and the Romanesque portals.

As you head onto the old town's main street, known to
the locals as Via Maestra, but officially Via Vittorio
Emanuele II, the air is redolent of roasting hazelnuts and
chocolate, wafting across from the Ferrero plant. This is
where the sticky Nutella spread is produced – 'mother love
in a jar' as the advertising slogan puts it. Less sickly perhaps are the famous Ferrero Rocher chocolates, also produced here. And, during October and the first two weekends
of November, noses are tickled by an altogether more pungent and complex scent at the market devoted to the prized
white truffle. Giacomo Morra is the man who did much to
popularise the white truffle in the 1950s and 1960s when he
began the tradition of sending a sample of this expensive
fungus to celebrities and statesmen.

The Via Maestra continues past food shops and smart boutiques up to the Piazza Savona which is 19th-century neoclassical in style and separates the old from the new town. In the middle of the piazza is a fountain which was presented to the town by the Ferrero family in 1972 when the company became quoted on the stock exchange.

Grinzane Cavour

The road out of Alba winds 5km (3 miles) south-west to **Grinzane Cavour**, which is divided into two villages. Gallo is the more industrial of the two, site of Piedmont's largest producer of *torrone* (nougat). Perched on the hill is the more historic half of this double act, Grinzane, dominated by its medieval castle, **Castello di Grinzane Cavour** (Via Cavour 5; tel: 0173-262 159; open Wed–Mon, Dec and Feb–Aug 9.30am–12.30pm and 2.30–6.30pm; daily Sept–Nov – hours as above). The Piedmontese statesman Camillo Benso, Count of Cavour (also the mayor of Grinzane for 17 years), used this as his country mansion in the 19th century. Well worth a visit is the 16th-century Mask Room whose ceiling is painted with portraits, crests, fantasy monsters, allegories and animals. The Ethnographic Museum here displays some of Cavour's personal effects and represents an authentic picture of life from the 17th to 19th centuries. Look for the Roman finds on the wines produced in the area and the informative panels on the white truffle.

This is also the site of the white truffles auction, held every year at the end of October or beginning of November, when vast sums of money are exchanged for the 'white gold'. It is open by invitation only. Open to everyone, however, is the excellent restaurant serving typical Piedmontese cuisine and the Enoteca Regionale Piemontese Cavour – one of the finest regional wine cellars, with an extensive collection of Piedmontese wines and grappa.

Barolo

The road continues south-west past gentle hills and slopes covered with vineyards and dotted with medieval fortresses. Just 3km (2 miles) from Gallo, lying on a plateau and surrounded by hills, is the village of **Barolo**.

Overlooking this picture-postcard scene is the **Castello dei Marchesi Falletti di Barolo** (Piazza Falletti, tel: 0173-562 77; open Fri–Wed 10am–12.30pm and 3–6.30pm; closed Jan; admission fee). The story of Barolo, the 'king of wines', began at this castle, which dates from the 10th century. Around 1250, a powerful family of bankers, the Falletti from Alba, bought it, together with all the surrounding land which they managed until 1864. From this land the first Barolo wine was produced on the initiative of the Marquise Juliette Colbert Falletti. Following the death of her husband, Carlo Falletti, in 1838, she decided to make a hobby out of her love of French red wine aged in oak casks. Using Nebbiolo grapes, she aged her wine for seven years in chestnut-wood barrels to give a full-bodied flavour. Naming her wine after the village, she presented King Carlo Alberto with 325 casks of it – one cask for each day of the year except the 40 days of Lent. And so the 'king of wines' was

The king of wines

born. Inside the castle the history of Barolo wine is told, and in the cellars you can try the wine for yourself.

From here, a very pleasant short drive north passes vine-clad hills to **La Morra**, one of the 11 towns that make up the area where Barolo is produced. From the main **Piazza Castello** there are outstanding views over the Langhe and the Alps, dotted with little towns, castles and towers surveying the surrounding vineyards.

North-west of here is **Pollenzo**, site of the world's first University of Taste, and **Bra**, birthplace of the Slow Food Movement *(see below)*.

Il Monferrato

Along with Le Langhe, this area forms the heartland of Piedmont's gastronomic and wine-growing country. Lying to the

---

The Slow Food Movement

The Slow Food Movement was born in Bra in Piedmont in 1986 and is dedicated to countering fast-food culture. Its manifesto urges us to 'rediscover the flavours and savours of regional cooking and banish the degrading effects of fast food'. The movement now has more than 80,000 members spread across five continents.

Every other year in October, a huge food fair known as the Salone del Gusto is held by the movement at the Lingotto complex in Turin. The movement's latest venture is much more ambitious – the University of Gastronomic Science. This is the world's first institution to elevate food and drink to an academic discipline, with three-year degree courses. The syllabus is purely to educate the palate, not to learn how to cook. The movement's president, Carlo Petrini, explains that the aim is 'to create a new food culture and to train students intent on its mastery'. The campus is a beautiful, restored palazzo at Pollenza, near Bra (Piazza Vittorio Emanuele 9, 12042-Pollenzo-Bra; tel: 0172-458 511; <www.unisg.it>).

north-east of Le Langhe, it is made up of the area between the rivers Po and Tanaro, known as Basso (low) Monferrato, and the area from the Tanaro to the Ligurian border, Alto (high) Monferrato. It is an idyllic hilly landscape scattered with vineyards, woods and farmsteads, and where almost every rise is crowned by country houses, churches, towers and ruins.

On parade during Asti's Palio

Asti

In the heart of the area is **Asti** – a city of narrow streets, graceful churches and medieval towers. The highlight is the 14th-century cathedral, one of Piedmont's finest Gothic buildings. The **Cattedrale di Santa Maria Assunta** (open daily 8.30am–noon and 3.30–5.30pm) has a lovely portico of tufa and brick. Inside, there are 17th-century frescoes.

Asti's central **Piazza Alfieri** resounds to the thundering of hooves in late September during the **Palio d'Asti** – a horse race similar to the one held in Siena. This event coincides with the local wine fair, reflecting Asti's renoun for producing sweet Asti Spumante (sparkling wine made from Moscato grapes) and its central position in Italy's most important wine-making region. Many other kinds of wine, from Dolcetto to Barbera, can be tasted in wineries throughout the area.

South of Asti is **Canelli**, one of Italy's wine capitals and site of the Underground Wine Cathedral. Kilometres of vaulted brick tunnels winding beneath the town create an atmospheric setting. The most prestigious wines of Canelli age in these 'naves' at a constant temperature of 12–14°C (54–57°F). In 1895, half of all the Moscato in Piedmont was cultivated and sold in the Borough of Canelli alone. In the 20th century, the international fortunes of Asti led to the expansion of the zone of origin, but Canelli still boasts the title 'capital of Asti and Moscato'. One top wine producer, **Coppo** (Via Alba 68; tel: 0141-823 146; tours by appointment; open every third weekend in Sept, Oct and Nov), has been in the same family since 1892. Having virtually abandoned sparkling wine production, it lists the delicious red Barbera d'Asti as its leading product.

Nearby is the **Gancia** winery (Corso Libertà 66; tel: 0141-83011; open daily 9am–12.30pm and 3–6.30pm; reservations only, tel: 0141-830 212). Around 6 percent of all Asti Spumante is produced here, as are many other wines and aperitifs, including vermouth and even a home brand of gin. Within the cellars is an *infernotto* – a small but fascinating museum charting the history of Gancia from the days when it started to produce Italy's first sparkling wine over 150 years ago. There is also a well-stocked bar for tastings.

MOUNTAINS AND VALLEYS TO THE WEST

Fabled landscapes are just an hour's car journey from Turin. Spectacular valleys studded with fortresses and sites of pilgrimage give way to the majesty of the Alps, sprinkled with traditional mountain villages and snowy playgrounds.

Val di Susa

To the west of Turin lies the Val di Susa, the old route between France and Italy once known as the Via Francigena (Frankish Route). The high mountains bordering these countries deterred neither Hannibal in 218BC nor the Saracen pirates of the Middle Ages nor, much later, the Spanish and French.

As a result, the area bristles with forts, castles and sites of pilgrimage. At the valley's entrance stands the **Sacra di San Michele** (Via alla Sacra 14, Sant'Ambrogio; tel: 011-939 130; open mid-Mar–mid-Oct Tues–Sun 9.30am–noon and 3–6pm; mid-Oct–mid-Mar until 5pm; Sat evenings in Aug; admission fee), which is accessible by the A32 motorway from Turin. Visible from afar, this imposing monastery clings to the peak of Monte Pirchiriano, 962m (3,156ft) high, and there is a steep climb to the entrance. Begun in the late 10th century for the Benedictine monks on the Via Francigena – the pilgrimage route to Rome – it became an important study centre and was enlarged many times until the Benedictine order was forced out in 1622.

Now in the hands of the Rosminian fathers, the abbey is Gothic in appearance and, after major work in the 1990s, it has been restored to its former glory. The highlights here

Sacra di San Michele

include the **Porta dello Zodiaco**, a door adorned with marble bas reliefs of the signs of the zodiac carved by 12th-century sculptor Nicolao; the **Scalone dei Morti** (Staircase of the Dead), a reference to the tombs of the monks of which five are now visible; and the **Torre della Bell'Alda**, the tower from which a local beauty, Alda, threw herself to escape from a soldier. Perhaps most spectacular of all are the views from the Belvedere Terrace.

Continuing west along the A32, the route leads to **Susa**, from which the valley takes its name. Known to the Romans as Segusium, the origins of Susa are easy to spot in the **Arco di Augusto** and **Anfiteatro** (open daily 7.30am–8pm) in a park just outside the centre of the old town. The arch and amphitheatre were built in honour of Emperor Augustus between 9 and 8BC in what was the Roman forum. Standing on a peak above the town is **Castello di Adelaide**, given to Countess Adelaide by her husband Oddone in the 11th century. Within the old town, the **Porta Savoia** gate, once part of the Roman defence system, is now joined to the **Cattedrale San Giusto** (Piazza San Giusto; open daily 7am–6pm, closed Sun lunchtime). Built in the 11th century, it has a Romanesque bell tower and exceptional 14th-century wooden choir stalls.

Towards the mountains, 12km (7½ miles) from Susa, is the beginning of the **Alta** (upper) **Val di Susa** and the little medieval town of **Exilles**, spectacularly located in a rocky valley. The town's fort is home to the **Museo delle Truppe Alpine e delle Fortificazioni delle Alpi Occidentali** (Via degli Alpini; tel: 0122-58270; open mid-Apr–Sept Tues–Sun 10am–7pm, Oct–mid Apr 10am–2pm; admission fee). A fort has watched over the passage between Italy and France from at least the 12th century, but today's imposing structure overlooking the lower Susa valley dates mainly from the early 19th century. The museum charts the fort's long history and the story of Italy's alpine troops. Don't miss the

The fort at Exilles

Knights' Courtyard and the Staircase of Paradise leading to the Prison Courtyard. This was the prison home of the enigmatic 'Man in the Iron Mask' from 1681 to 1687.

Winter Resorts

The Upper Val di Susa and adjoining Chisone Valley together form one of the top areas in the Alps for snow sports. The **Via Lattea** (Milky Way) is a snowy paradise of 400km (250 miles) of linked ski pistes, key sites for the 2006 Winter Olympics. The winter season here starts around the first week of December and finishes after Easter, while the summer season is from early June to mid-September – the perfect time for outdoor pursuits in the warm, mountain air. Spring and autumn are off-season, and even though the weather may be beautiful many hotels and restaurants will be closed. Easily accessible by car from Turin on the fast A32, once you start the ascent into the mountains, conditions can be treacherous

Sestriere ski resort

and snow chains will be needed on many of the passes. There are regular train services to resorts such as Bardonecchia and Sauze d'Oulz from Turin.

Host to alpine skiing competitions, snow-sure **Sestriere** sits at an altitude of 2,000m (6,560ft) on a sunny plateau. This was the first purpose-built resort in the Alps, created by Fiat's Giovanni Agnelli in the 1930s. Dismayed that his family went abroad to ski, he created a 'home from home' ski resort, convenient to Turin.

Sestriere is the Milky Way's smartest resort, despite its concrete architecture. It's a great base for exploring the Via Lattea and features the most challenging skiing in the entire region, although there's plenty for confident intermediates and some nursery slopes. During the summer you could swap skis for golf clubs, if you want to play on Europe's highest golf course.

Sauze d'Oulx (1,510m/4,950ft; Olympic venue for freestyle skiing), also linked to the Via Lattea, is an attractive old town with a tangle of cobbled streets. The main part, close to the slopes, buzzes with sports bars. Its split personality is reflected in the origins of its residents: second-home owners from Turin, and the British on a budget. There is a good selection of uncrowded, open and tree-lined runs – good for all weather conditions – and some excellent mountain restaurants. Nearby is the small resort of **Cesana Sansicario** (1,700m/2,735ft; Olympic venue for women's downhill, super-G and biathlon). Popular with families, it is directly linked to Sauze d'Oulx and Sestriere.

To the north-west, near the entrance to the Fréjus Tunnel, is the old railway town of **Bardonecchia** (1,310m/4,300ft; Olympic venue for snowboard competitions). Especially suited to intermediate skiers and snowboarders, the area covers 140km (87 miles) of pistes, but is not connected to the Via Lattea. Julius Caesar's Roman legions passed through here in 58BC on their way to conquer Gaul.

To the east, **Pragelato** (Olympic venue for ski jumping, cross-country skiing and Nordic combined competitions) has 50km (31 miles) of trails and is well suited to snowshoeing. It has the highest ski jump in the world.

To the south-east, at the entrance to Val Chisone, is the attractive town of **Pinerolo** (Olympic venue for curling), with an old centre and a fine 15-century cathedral.

AROUND MONTE ROSA

In the northern part of Piedmont, on the border with Switzerland, stands Monte Rosa, at 3,500m (11,500ft) the Alps' second highest mountain after Mont Blanc.

Monterosa Ski

Encompassing the resorts of Champoluc, Gressoney and Alagna, **Monterosa Ski** is also popular with lovers of winter sports, though it is less extensive than the Via Lattea.

Set in the Valsesia Valley, **Alagna** is a cult area for expert off-piste skiing, with

Since the 13th century, the Valsesia area has been home to the Walsers, a German-speaking people. The Walsers have traditionally practised sophisticated woodworking skills, and their social structure is as robust as their houses.

some of the Alps' toughest skiing. However, a new 100-person cable car from Alagna and a new piste to Gressoney and Alagna have opened up the area to less intrepid skiers, and both **Champoluc** and **Gressoney** have long, cruising intermediate runs. Slopes here are usually quiet and the snow is reliable. The landscape is dotted with unspoilt, traditional villages.

In Pedemonte ('z'Kantmud'), a tiny hamlet a few minutes' walk from Alagna, the **Museo Walser** (tel: 0347-137 7404; open Sept–Jun Sat, Sun and hols 2–6pm; Jul daily 2–6pm; Aug daily 10am–noon and 2–6pm) gives an insight into the lifestyle of the Walser – the valley's German-speaking inhabitants – in a three-storey house built in 1628.

Varallo's Sacro Monte

Some 40km (25 miles) down the valley from Alagna is the picturesque town of **Varallo**, with cobbled streets and manor houses overlooked by the spectacular **Sacro Monte** (tel: 0163-51131; open at all times; free; guided tours available at the local tourism office, tel: 0163-564 404).

In 1481, a Franciscan friar named Bernardino Caimi returned from Jerusalem in search of a suitable spot to create a miniature Holy Land in the West. He found in Varallo an ideal setting. By 1493 three chapels had been erected on the mount. Now there are 43 chapels, each depicting scenes with life-like statues and frescoes, many of which are by the masterful 16th-century artist, Gaudenzio Ferrari. A fountain in the piazza takes the place of Chapel 44, and is made from a single piece of rock,

A *sacro monte* (sacred mountain) is a collection of chapels on a hillside, usually representing the Stations of the Cross. Of the nine *sacri monti* in this region of northern Italy, Varallo's is the oldest and most important and was listed as a UNESCO World Heritage Site in 2003.

The façade of the basilica at Varallo's Sacro Monte

crowned by the statue of Christ Risen. The basilica here was commissioned in 1614, but not completed until the end of the 19th century. Above the altar is a majestic dome, decorated with angels, prophets and cherubs. Look also for the image of the Sleeping Virgin – the Madonna of the Sacro Monte.

Biella

Driving south from Varallo towards Turin, you come to the province of **Biella**, also known as the Textile or Cashmere Valley. This is Europe's main textile manufacturing centre and home to over 200 mills, producing cashmere, worsted fabrics and mohair. Ermenegildo Zegna founded a mill here in 1910 and the family now has a 30 percent share of the world's luxury menswear market, supplying labels such as Valentino and Gucci. The factories of Biella account for 65 percent of Italian output. You can visit more than 50 factory outlets or *spaccio* located along the SS230.

WHAT TO DO

This city of a thousand faces and a thousand tastes has delights and surprises around every corner. You'll find fabulous shopping in the chic boutiques under the colonnades and, if you can't afford to buy, you can at least spend time window-shopping. Or go to a market – the one at Porta Palazzo is the largest in Europe – if only for the people-watching. Have a taste of *la dolce vita* in one of the city's historic cafés over a delicious chocolate *bicerin* – a speciality of Turin – and don't forget *aperitivo* time in the evening, the social highlight of the day. Then, as night falls, there's everything from opera to street theatre, classical music to rock, ethnic eateries to gourmet restaurants. After dinner, the bars along the Po are open until dawn. Away from the city, Piedmont's food and drink make tempting souvenirs, and then there are the Alps, beckoning skiers and hikers alike. And there's plenty to keep the little ones amused too.

SPORTS

Winter Sports

Facilities for winter sports are highly developed, and not just in the Alps. The city itself has several ice-skating rinks where skates can be hired at a modest price. The most popular skiing and snowboarding locations are about an hour's drive to the west at the resorts of the Via Lattea (Milky Way), covering 600km (370 miles) of slopes. Sestriere offers excellent facilities, plus more challenging grades of skiing; Sauze d'Oulx has a split personality,

Off-piste skiing in Alagna

catering for weekending Torinesi and foreign tourists alike; Bardonecchia is both pretty and well suited to families. North of Turin, close to the Swiss border, and hard up against Monte Rosa (the highest mountain in the Alps after Mont Blanc) are the intermediate areas of Gressoney and Champoluc, while Alagna is the fabled destination for serious off-piste enthusiasts.

Even if downhill skiing and snowboarding are not to your taste, there are plenty of opportunities for cross-country skiing and snow-shoeing, both of which are great ways to enjoy the high mountain scenery.

Other Outdoor Activities

Italians love **cycling** and Turin has over 40km (25 miles) of cycle paths. Several hotels hire out bikes; the tourist information centre in the AtriumTorino hires bikes free of charge to tourists. There are some lovely rides along the riverbank, as well as through the main parks of Valentino, Mandria and Pellerina.

Running is also becoming increasingly popular. You will see joggers hard at work in the parks every morning and evening and at weekends. Turin's annual marathon in April

---

Park Life

The French architect Le Corbusier praised Turin as 'the city with the most beautiful natural location'. The proximity of the Alps accounts for some of that beauty, but a significant part comes from Turin's extensive parks and gardens, and its hundreds of kilometres of tree-lined streets. In total there are 17 parks, and the new Parco della Dora will eventually provide another 45 hectares (110 acres) of greenery for the Torinesi. It's no wonder that for many this is Italy's greenest city.

A packed-out Juventus crowd at the Stadio delle Alpi

is one of Italy's most famous and most picturesque. Of the riverside parks, Valentino and della Colletta have especially scenic trails and are popular with runners of all standards. A jog in the Parco Cavalieri di Vittorio Veneto gives the added attraction of perhaps getting a glimpse over the fence of the Juventus football team being put through their paces.

In summer there is some superb **climbing** and **hiking** in the areas around Monte Rosa, including relatively easy day walks. The Club Alpino Italiano can give more information: <www.caitorino.it>.

Football fever runs high in Turin, no more so than when Juventus locks horns with its rivals, the Torino team. Juventus, known as 'the old lady of Turin', is the older of the city's two teams and the more famous, currently on top of Serie A, while Torino languishes below in Serie B. The season runs from September to May and matches are held at the modern Stadio delle Alpi, about 30 minutes from the city centre. Built for the 1999 World Cup, this stadium has more than 70,000 seats. Tickets can be bought from lotto ticket sellers, some tobacconists, ticket offices or through the teams' websites: Juventus Club, <www.juventus.com>; Torino Calcio, <www.toro.it>.

Although still an exclusive game in Italy, **golf** is very popular in Turin. Turismo Torino at the AtriumTorino sells one- and three-day golf passes, which can be used on most of the courses in and around Turin; passes include the use of a bag and clubs. The closest course is at Stupinigi. The ski resort of Sestriere is home to Europe's highest golf course – at an altitude of 2,000m (6,560ft).

Teatro Regio

Among other sports, there are good **riding** stables at Moncalieri, La Mandria, Venaria and at Stupinigi, where there is also horse racing, and the city has about 10 open-air **swimming** pools; regulations require you to wear a swim cap at these pools.

ENTERTAINMENT

From October to June, the Teatro Regio (Piazza Castello 215; tel: 011-881 5241; <www.teatroregiotorino.it>) runs a repertoire of **opera**, **classical ballet** and **concerts**. Tickets are at a premium, especially for first nights, and it is virtually impossible to be overdressed here. The theatre also organises a contemporary dance festival, TorinoDanza, (tel: 011-881 5259; <www.comune.torino/it/torinodanza>), held in various venues from September to November and in February and May. Contemporary dance is also staged at the Teatro Nuovo (Corso Massimo d'Azeglio 17; tel: 011-650 0211; <www.teatronuovo.torino.it>).

Music is both very varied and extremely high in quality. Performances by the RAI Symphony Orchestra are held twice weekly in the Lingotto at the Auditorium Giovanni Agnelli (Via Nizza, 280), which is also the venue for many of the events of the international Settembre Musica festival. The Conservatorio Giuseppe Verdi (Via Mazzini 11; tel: 011-817 8458; <www.conservatorio-torino.it>) is a famous music school as well as the venue for concerts by the Orchestra Filarmonica di Torino and the Unione Musicale, featuring both foreign and Italian musicians and singers.

The city also has a lively avant-garde music scene. One well-established venue for concerts and theatre shows, as well as being a club on Saturday evenings, is Hiroshima Mon Amour (Via Bossoli 83, Lingotto; tel: 011-317 6636; <www.hiroshimamonamour.org>).

Among other music venues are Barrumba (Via San Massimo 1; tel: 011-819 4347; <www.barrumba.com>), which has live events and also organises summer festivals; and the Mazda Palace (Corso Ferrara 30,

Art comes to the streets of Turin at Christmas time in a dazzling display of light installations designed by famous international artists. Holograms, planetarium lights and bathtubs of volcanic red water are just some of these extraordinarily inventive displays. The exhibition changes every year and is a marvellous antidote to the usual Christmas fairy lights. The lights are switched on in November and turned off again in late January.

north-west suburbs; tel: 011-455 9090; <www.mazda palace.it>), which attracts big, internationally known names.

The jazz scene is vibrant in Turin, and the Centro Jazz Torino (tel: 011-884 477; <www.centrojazztorino.it>) promotes events such as Blues Al Femminile – showcasing female blues singers – in autumn and spring, and Linguaggi Jazz, which welcomes new and emerging artists, from January to March.

For those interested in **theatre**, the Teatro Stabile di Torino company, <www.teatrostabiletorino.it>, stages Italian and international classics in the lovely Teatro Carignano (Piazza Carignano 6; tel: 011-517 6246) and sometimes in the Teatro Alfieri. Hiroshima Mon Amour *(see page 87)* has a successful cabaret season from October to May. Some of the city's summer festivals – such as the Festival delle Colline, <www.festivaldellecolline.it> – put on performances in the gardens of private villas.

Featuring rock acts, the Traffic Torino Free Festival is held every July

Cinema and Nightlife

Turin has more cinema screens per capita than any other Italian city. However, most foreign-language films are dubbed into Italian. The Sala Massimo, near the Cinema Museum, screens experimental and foreign films, many in English.

The Museo Nazionale del Cinema housed in the Mole Antonelliana *(see page 51)* highlights Turin's long association with the cinematic arts (the city was the birthplace of the Italian film industry). The city honours this heritage by hosting the Torino Film Festival, held each year in November. This is the country's most important film festival after Venice, and over the years has been the launching pad of many a new talent.

The city has no shortage of bars, cafés, clubs, discos and other nightlife venues. The locals tend to start off the evening's entertainment with *aperitivi*, the local ritual of having a drink or two accompanied by a range of tasty appetisers. Whether it's a plush, historic café or a more modern establishment, everyone has a favourite place to enjoy *aperitivi* (for suggested bars and cafés, *see page 140*). Afterwards, the Quadrilatero Romano, north of Via Garibaldi, is the fashionable place to meet.

In summer the Murazzi embankment along the river has back-to-back clubs, converted from former boathouses. Prominent among them is The Beach, which has beach umbrellas and deckchairs by day, and Giancarlo, where the Murazzi nightscene first began over 20 years ago.

Other good places for nightlife are the Docks Dora, north-west of Porta Palazzo, formerly a very run-down area, and now the heart of the alternative scene (as distinct from the more commercial clubs). For entry to these venues you should be a member of the Italian AICS or ARCI cultural clubs, but the fee is normally waived for foreigners on presentation of a passport.

Porta Palazzo, Europe's largest open-air market

SHOPPING

Shops in Turin tend to open from 9.30am to 12.30pm and from 3.30 to 7.30pm, although an increasing number operate nonstop all day. Shops not specialising in food are normally closed on Monday mornings, while most small supermarkets and food shops are closed on Wednesday afternoons. The majority of shops close on Sunday, but there are exceptions such as shopping centres. Sunday trading becomes much more widespread during December's pre-Christmas rush.

Clothes

For **designer fashions**, the Via Roma is the city's most exclusive street, where shopping under the porticoes is a weather-protected, although rather expensive, pleasure. Armani and Hermès are here, along with the more modestly priced Zara and Mango outlets and the Upim department store. Nearby, in Via Lagrange, is La Rinascente – a more upmarket department store with everything from cosmetics to fashions and tableware. Young designers, producing clothes with strikingly individualistic styles, have colonised the Via Bonelli in the Quadrilatero Romano.

For **cheaper boutiques** and **chain stores**, head for the Via Garibaldi. This pedestrianised precinct is particularly good for **leather accessories**, but also try Bertolini & Borse in Piazza Vittorio Veneto for its huge selection of shoes, bags and other leather goods.

Markets can be a good source of inexpensive finds, whether new or second-hand. The best location for clothes and shoes is the Crocetta market in Via Marco Polo in the Crocetta district.

Specialist Shops

Plenty of specialist shops are dotted around the city. You can find them all under one roof at the Porta Palazzo – Europe's largest open-air market. And for lovers of **antiques and bric-a-brac**, the Balôn market in the Borga Dora is the place to be on a Saturday. Its big cousin, the Gran Balôn, takes place in the same location on the second Sunday in the month.

If you are on the lookout for more expensive antiques, try the shops of the Via della Rocca, Via Bogino, Via Principe Amedeo and Via Maria Vittoria.

Galleria Subalpina

For antique and **second-hand books**, the Via Po is hard to beat, while shops in the Galleria Subalpina off the Piazza Castello offer an excellent selection of rare maps and prints.

For **sports** enthusiasts, Juventus has a shop in Via Garibaldi, while Torino has shops in Via Costa and Via Allioni. Turin has several shops selling souvenirs of the Winter Olympics located at the Atrium Torino, the airport and along the Via Garibaldi.

Wood carving is a craft that has been practised in the Piedmontese valleys for many centuries. Bardonecchia, in the mountains, is home to a wood-carving school. Good buys include everything from the smallest kitchen utensils to grand pieces of furniture.

Wood carving on display in the Museo Walser in Alagna

Gourmet Treats

In this city of **chocolate** it would be sacrilege not to take home some *gianduiotti* chocolates. The display in the windows of the confectioner's Stratta at Piazza San Carlo – with every sweet delight from *marrons glacés* to darkest chocolate – is literally good enough to eat. And for real chocolate addicts, Peyrano in Corso Vittorio Emanuele II has no less than 90 different types to choose from.

But **Piedmontese cuisine** is, of course, much more than this. Gourmet treats such as locally produced wines, cheeses, hams and salamis, fine quality olive oil, white truffles and *grissini* (Turin's very own breadsticks) all make lovely souvenirs.

CHILDREN

In all but the smartest, most expensive restaurants, children are welcomed with open arms, just as they are in the rest of Italy. And don't forget the city's many cafés, for chocolate and gelato treats.

The Museo Nazionale del Cinema is virtually guaranteed to delight with its hands-on displays and film sequences. Children are bound to find the panoramic lift to the top of the Mole Antonelliana (which houses the museum) excitingly breathtaking.

A favourite with the city's children is the funicular railway ride up to the Basilica di Superga. Down in the city, a stroll around the Parco del Valentino is a nice way to while away the time, and the park's medieval village and fortress are good for active exploration. During the summer there are free puppet shows in the park on Sunday afternoon. The puppet museum, Museo della Marionetta, has a fascinating collection of more than 5,000 string and hand puppets, for those keen to learn more about the ancestors of Punch and Judy. Experimenta, in the Parco Michelotti, is a fun, interactive scientific exhibition in the former zoo area.

Summer is the time for a dip in an outdoor swimming pool. During the winter, the snowy playground of the Alps is the perfect place for children to let off steam.

A sure-fire way to please the little ones

Festivals

January *Sintonie*, Turin – festival of music, theatre, cinema and visual arts.

February *Carnevale*, Turin, Rivoli and Ivrea – the beginning of Lent is celebrated with parades and shows. *CioccolaTO*, Turin (Feb–Mar) – celebration of chocolate.

March *Musica 90*, Turin – music concerts from different regions.

April *Turin Marathon. Settimana dei Beni Culturali* – Cultural Heritage Week with free admission to all public museums. *Da Sodoma a Hollywood*, Turin – one of Europe's top gay and lesbian film festivals.

May *Fiera Internazionale del Libro*, Turin – five-day book fair at Lingotto.

June *Processione della Consolata*, Turin (20 June) – procession of the Madonna from the Chiesa della Consolata. *Festa di San Giovanni*, Turin (24 June) – festival of the patron saint, St John, with regattas and fireworks on the River Po. *Assedio di Canelli*, Canelli, near Asti (third weekend of June) – re-enactment of the siege of 1613 by Mantuan forces.

July *Traffic Torino Free Festival* – rock festival. *Sentinelle delle Alpi* – music, shows, cinema and theatrical events in the forts of Exilles and Fenestrelle.

August *Mostra Mercato dell'Artigianato*, Pinerolo – handicrafts fair.

September *Torino Settembre Musica* – classical music festival. *Douja d'Or* and *Palio*, Asti – wine and grappa fair culminating in the bareback horseride, the Palio d'Asti. *Festa del Barolo*, Barolo (2nd weekend) – grape harvest festival. *Le Forme del Latte*, Bra (third weekend in odd-numbered years) – fine cheese fair organised by the Slow Food Movement.

October *Salone Internazionale del Gusto*, Turin (every two years) – food fair organised by the Slow Food Movement. *Fiera Nazionale del Tartufo Bianco d'Alba* (second to third week) – Alba celebrates the prized white truffle with events including tasting courses and concerts.

November *Torino Film Festival. Artissima*, Turin – international exhibition of contemporary art. *Luci d'Artista*, Turin (Nov–Jan) – spectacular light installations created by world-acclaimed artists illuminate Turin's piazzas, streets and monuments.

December *Christmas Markets*, Turin. *Capodanno*, Piazza San Carlo, Turin – New Year's Eve celebrations.

EATING OUT

Italian food is revered throughout the world and, if imitation is the sincerest form of flattery, it is probably also the world's best-loved cuisine. But to enjoy authentic *cucina italiana*, you have to sample it in the country of its birth. However, you should bear in mind that there is, in fact, no such thing as Italian food, rather a mixture of different regional dishes.

When in Piedmont, prepare yourself for rich, robust flavours, laced with French flair – reflecting the region's historic relationship with the royal house of Savoy – and indulge yourself in gourmet delicacies fit for a king.

A Piedmontese selection

WHERE TO EAT

For breakfast *(prima colazione)* pop into a café for a cappuccino, espresso or caffè latte and a brioche. Do as the locals do and consume them at the counter. If you sit down it is invariably more expensive, especially if you sit outside. Alternatively, breakfast may be included in the price of your accommodation.

If you want a light lunch there are plenty of cafés, bars, wine bars *(enoteche)* and pizza houses *(pizzerie)* from which to choose. Italian *caffès* also serve alcoholic drinks and may stock *latteria* (dairy produce), *pasticceria* (cakes) or *gelateria* (ice cream). If you want to buy ingredients for a picnic, go to a *salumeria* (delicatessen) or a *tavola calda*, which serves sandwiches *(tramezzini)* and cold or hot dishes.

In Turin's historic cafés there are still many locals who take tea or the delicious *bicerin* (a chocolate/hazelnut drink that is a speciality of the city) in the afternoon. In the early evening, cafés and bars throughout the city are packed with people enjoying the social highlight of the day, *aperitivo* time. *Aperitivi* are accompanied by increasingly vast buffets, which are included in the price of your drink. Many people indulge so much in these snacks that they simply do not have room for dinner afterwards. But assuming that your appetite is aroused, not sated, there is no shortage of excellent eateries to try.

Restaurants *(ristoranti)* are usually the most expensive and formal option, but the cheaper *osterie* or *trattorie*, with less luxurious surroundings, often serve some of the best food in town. However, overall prices for food in Turin tend to be extremely competitive in comparison with those in many other Italian cities, so it should not cost a king's ransom to dine like a monarch here.

> It is customary to round off your restaurant bill with a tip in addition to the service charge, as this is something that the waiter does not usually receive.

In Turin and the surrounding area a number of restaurants have introduced *le tavole del sapore* – tasting menus. A *menu del sapore* gives a taste of regional gourmet cuisine and includes two courses, a dessert or cheese and mineral water at a fixed price, which is usually excellent value.

Elegant Caffè San Carlo

WHAT TO EAT

Antipasti

The *antipasto* – the Italian version of *hors d'oeuvre* – is a very important part of Piedmontese cuisine. Pickled and cooked vegetables are a popular regional speciality, known as *bagna caôda*. This is a warm, aromatic mixture of olive oil, butter, anchovies and garlic, to which milk, cream or truffles are added and into which raw vegetables are dipped. It is also often served simply poured over peppers – *peperoni con bagna cauda* (or *bagna caôda*).

Anchovies *(acciughe)* are used in a variety of dishes, such as in the preparation of peppers, which may be stuffed with rice, butter, garlic, oil and anchovies and cooked in the oven, but served cold. Although this is a land-locked area, the long tradition of trade with neighbouring Liguria on the Mediterranean has made these little silver fish, along with olive oil

Vitello tonnato

and capers, into staple ingredients of the cuisine.

A classic Piedmontese dish, *vitello tonnato* is a surprisingly delicious blend of cold roast veal and tuna served with a mayonnaise sauce with gherkins and capers. A type of dry-cured beef known as *bresaola* and other raw meats also feature marinated in oil, garlic and lemon juice, while salamis such as *mustardela* from Valle Pellice are robust and spicy.

Little cheeses are often served with spicy sauce as *antipasti*, including castelmagno cheese with *cognà* (chutney). Snails *(lumache)* are also a delicacy, especially in the Cherasco area where they are served either with butter and garlic or in a tomato, olive oil and garlic sauce.

Every restaurant table will come dressed with *grissini*, the breadsticks that are reputed to have first been made for Vittorio Amedeo II in Turin in the late 1600s. Some traditions never die.

Primi

The first course *(il primo)* is the staple of any meal in a country that believes that not only is pasta delicious but also vital to nutrition. You will receive sad looks if you decide to miss out on this course. But there are other variations of the pasta course, too, especially rice from the local paddy fields of

Vercelli, the rice capital of Europe. And then there's polenta, made of yellow maize and often served as an accompaniment to dishes as well as on its own as a *primo*.

The favourite Piedmontese pasta is *agnolotti* – crescent-shaped ravioli stuffed with meat or vegetables; these are served with *ragù* (meat and tomato sauce) or creamy sauces. Also popular is *tajarin* – long, flat pasta made of egg and similar to thin tagliatelle; this is usually served with a meat sauce. Other varieties include little pasta discs known as *cruset*; these are rather similar to *orecchiette*, which are in the shape of little ears (hence the name) and come from Puglia. Toppings include the simple *burro e salvia* (butter and sage), sauces made with Piedmontese cheeses such as toma and ricotta or with wild mushrooms – or, most lavishly, with slivers of truffle. A risotto scented with truffles, especially the prized white variety from Alba, is Piedmont cuisine at its most splendid.

> **Other classic Italian pasta sauces include** *all'arrabbiata* **(tomato and chilli),** *all'amatriciana* **(a spicy concoction of tomato, sausage chilli and onion),** *al pesto* **(basil, pine nuts and pecorino cheese) and** *alle vongole* **(with clams).**

Secondi

The main dish in Italy is known as *il secondo*. Carnivores will be in their element in Piedmont, as many dishes are meat based. But there is plenty of fish too, including saltwater fish from Liguria and fresh fish from local rivers and lakes. Swordfish, trout, turbot, sea bass, salmon, sardines, oysters, octopus, prawns, lobsters and many other fishy delights feature on menus. The local delicacy of frogs' legs comes from the rice fields of Vercelli and is often served, aptly, with risotto.

Piedmont also produces Italy's greatest red wines, and the prized Barolo and Barbaresco varieties frequently feature as a marinade in beef recipes. *Fritto misto alla piemontese* is a mixture of breaded, fried meats and vegetables contrasting salty with sweet flavours. The dish normally includes chicken, pork, veal, liver and other offal, courgettes and apple. Veal and kid are also widely eaten, and raw meat is often served in the form of *carne all'albese* – veal served with olive oil and lemon, shavings of Parmesan cheese and (depending on the season and the depth of your pocket), sometimes slivers of white truffle. *Osso buco* – shin of veal braised slowly in wine – is also very popular. However, the standout for meat lovers is *bollito misto*. This rich dish usually includes seven varieties of boiled meat, always featuring calf's head and accompanied by as many different sauces.

White truffles from Alba

Contorni, vegetable side dishes, may include mushrooms, especially the prized *porcini* (boletus mushrooms), peppers, courgettes, spinach and many more.

Formaggi

Cheese *(formaggi)* is big in Piedmont. Just as the lush pastureland produces some of the country's best meat, it is also responsible for many of Italy's finest cheeses. Perhaps the best known of these is *gorgonzola*, available either as *piccante* (crumbly) or *dolce* (creamy), but always strong and blue.

Other varieties of Pied-
montese cheese include the
hard *toma* from the mountain valleys, soft goat's
cheeses such as *caprini*, and
ricotta. Try the *seirass del
Fen*, which is matured in
hay. *Fontina* is a rich, semi-
soft chewy mountain cheese
and *raschera* is a mixture of
cow's, sheep's and goat's
milk from Monferrato. *Fon-
duta*, a cheese fondue, is

***Toma* cheese**

usually made from fontina cheese and is especially delicious when combined with the white truffle.

Dolci

Slimmers beware, as the sublime sweets *(dolci)* in this region will test even the strongest of resolves. Hazelnut trees
blanket the countryside, and the fruits of the trees find their
way into many delicious puddings such as *torta nocciola* – a
light cake made with hazelnuts, eggs, butter and flour. The
ingot-shaped *gianduiotti*, studded with hazelnuts, are every
chocoholic's idea of paradise, and chocolate puddings are
very popular, such as *bonet*, a rich chocolate crème caramel.
Zabaione, a light, frothy concoction of egg yolks, sugar and
Marsala wine, is also very popular. *Gelati* (ice cream) is excellent in Turin – especially the choc-ice known as *pinguino*;
the hazelnut-flavoured, milk-chocolate *gianduja* is sublime
with whipped cream.

Vini

The quality of the wines *(vini)* of Piedmont is matched only by
that of Tuscany. From the Langhe Hills comes the powerful,

Turin's *aperitivo* hour begins at 7pm

complex and full-bodied red *(rosso)* Barolo, known as the 'king of wines', which commands very high prices. Also from this area and made from the same Nebbiolo grapes is Barbaresco – a lighter, delicious wine, best drunk when it is five to 10 years old. Barbera is very drinkable and affordable and comes in both still and slightly fizzy *(frizzante)* versions. Of the whites *(vino bianco)*, sweet, sparkling Asti Spumante needs little introduction, but is surprisingly and deliciously different in its home territory from the versions recognised outside Italy. The less famous Moscato d'Asti is a low-alcohol dessert wine and is excellent. Still white wines are not as common to the region, but there are some good Gavi varieties.

As producers of vermouth, Turin and Piedmont were famous first with Carpano, maker of the drink since 1786. However, it was under the name Martini that vermouth shot to fame. For more on the Torinese love of pre-prandial beverages, *see page 104*.

MENU READER

To help you order...

I'd like to book a table	**Vorrei riservare un tavolo**
Do you have a table for two?	**Avete un tavolo per due?**
May we have the menu?	**Ci dà il menu, per favore?**
fixed-price menu	**il menu a prezzo fisso**
dish of the day	**il piatto del giorno**
wine list	**la lista dei vini**

I'd like a/some…	**Vorrei…**		
beer	**una birra**	pepper	**del pepe**
bread	**del pane**	potatoes	**delle patate**
butter	**del burro**	salad	**dell'insalata**
coffee	**un caffè**	salt	**del sale**
cream	**della panna**	soup	**una minestra**
fork	**una forchetta**	spoon	**un cucchiaio**
glass	**un bicchiere**	sugar	**dello zucchero**
ice cream	**un gelato**	tea	**un tè**
knife	**un coltello**	wine	**del vino**

...and read the menu

asparagi	asparagus	**cavolfiore**	cauliflower
baccalà	salt cod	**cernia**	grouper
bistecca	steak	**cervella**	brains
branzino, spigola	sea bass	**cinghiale**	wild boar
		cipolle	onions
brodetto	fish soup	**coniglio**	rabbit
calamari	squid	**crostacei**	shellfish
capra	goat	**fagioli**	haricot beans
capriolo/ cervo	venison	**fave**	broad beans
		fegato	liver
carciofi	artichokes	**frittelle**	fritters

funghi porcini	boletus mushrooms	**porri**	leeks
gamberi, gamberetti	prawns, shrimps	**radicchio**	red lettuce
		rombo	turbot
gelato	ice cream	**rughetta, rucola**	rocket
granchio	crab	**salmone**	salmon
indivia	endive	**salsicce**	sausages
lattuga	lettuce	**sarde**	sardines
lepre	hare	**scalogno**	shallots
maiale	pork	**seppie**	cuttlefish
manzo	beef	**sogliola**	sole
melanzane	aubergines	**spinaci**	spinach
merluzzo	cod	**stufato**	stew
ostriche	oysters	**tacchino**	turkey
patate	potatoes	**tartufo**	truffle
peperoncino	chilli	**tonno**	tuna
peperoni	peppers	**triglia**	red mullet
pesce spada	swordfish	**trota**	trout
piselli	peas	**verza**	cabbage
pollo	chicken	**vitello**	veal
polpo	octopus	**vongole**	clams
pomodori	tomatoes	**zucchini**	courgette

Aperitivo Hour

Turin is the birthplace of vermouth, which was created in the 18th century from Moscato wine, absinthe and bitter herbs; Cinzano and Martini followed. The city prides itself on being the home of *aperitivi*, when your favourite tipple (vermouth or not) is accompanied by feasts of canapés, cold meats, pastas, cheeses and so on. *Aperitivo* hour usually starts at 7pm and goes on till around 9pm – but sometimes much later. A selection of the best cafés and bars in which to try an aperitif is listed on page 140.

HANDY TRAVEL TIPS

An A–Z Summary of Practical Information

A

ACCOMMODATION (*alloggio*; see also RECOMMENDED HOTELS on page 129)

Turin has a wide range of accommodation, mostly in the medium to high category. Hotels *(alberghi)* are classified in five categories, graded from one to five stars, based on the amenities and comfort they offer. Prices tend to be lower than in other major Italian cities.

Turismo Torino (tel: 011-535 181; <www.turismotorino.org>) has up-to-date hotel information *(see page 128)*. They offer a free hotel and B&B booking service, but you must contact them no more than 48 hours in advance for hotels (last-minute reservation service) and one week in advance for B&Bs.

Outside Turin, there are some excellent *agriturismo* – farmhouse accommodation, which has become extremely popular in recent years – and *pensioni*. Ask at tourist offices for lists of these properties, or check the website <www.agriturismoinitalia.com>.

Do you have any vacancies?	**Avete camere libere?**
I'd like a single/double room	**Vorrei una camera singola/matrimoniale**
…with bath/shower/private toilet	**…con bagno/doccia/ gabinetto privato.**
What's the rate per night/week?	**Qual è il prezzo per una notte/una settimana?**

AIRPORT (*aeroporto*)

Turin's airport, the Sandro Pertini, is in Caselle, 16km (10 miles) north of the centre of the city, and is usually referred to as Caselle airport. For general tourist information, tel: 011-535 181 (daily 8.30am–10.30pm). For flight information, tel: 011-567 6361/2 (daily 6am–midnight); <www.aeroportoditorino.it>.

Inside the airport is the Turismo Torino information centre, airline ticket offices and car-hire desks, and duty-free shopping for travellers from outside the EU. Travel by car or taxi to the city centre takes about 30 minutes. The taxi rank is at the arrivals level of the airport by the exit. There is an express train service into Turin operated by GTT (tel: 800-990 097, <www.gtt.to.it>), leaving every half-hour with a journey time of 20 minutes into Dora station in the north of Turin. The line is being extended into the more central Porta Susa station (which is to become the main railway hub, eventually replacing Porta Nuova). In the meantime, frequent Line 11 trains connect Dora to Porta Nuova.

The Sadem blue bus company (tel: 011-300 0611, <www. sadem.it>) has regular services to Porta Nuova departing from outside the airport's arrivals lounge. Buses leave approximately every 30 minutes and the trip takes about 40 minutes (for fare details, *see below*). Tickets are available from the ticket office in the airport. Note that there is a 50-cent surcharge if you buy a ticket on board the bus.

What time does the train/bus leave for the city centre?	**A che ora parte il treno/pullman per il centro?**

B

BUDGETING FOR YOUR TRIP

The following are average prices, based on high-season rates:

Airport transfer: Taxis charge €0.50 per bag and the average ride from the airport costs around €35, depending on the time of day. By train a single ticket costs €3, valid for 70 minutes, and allows use of trams and buses in the city too. A 24-hour ticket, giving unlimited travel, costs €5.50. Sadem bus tickets cost €5. Note that prices for train and bus travel to and from the airport are discounted for Torino Card holders (*see page 108*).

Camping: Average €4 per tent; €25 per camper/caravan per night.

Car hire: From €85 per day or €284 per week with unlimited mileage.

Entertainment: Cinema €7; concert from €5 for a Settembre Musica event up to €155 at the Teatro Regio.

Guides: (up to 25 people) in English €110 half day (bus not included); €220 full day.

Guided tours: A guide for one museum (for example Rivoli): 1–15 people in English €80; 16–25 people in English €100.

Meals and drinks: Continental breakfast €4–15; lunch/dinner in fairly good establishment €25–40; coffee €0.85 at the bar, €1.50–2 served at the table; carafe of house wine from €4; beer €1.50; soft drink €1.50; aperitif €2–4, but with *aperitivi* about €6.

Museums: Average €5, but see note on Torino Card below.

Petrol: €1.60 per litre.

Taxi: Meters start at €3.10 and from 10pm–7am a night surcharge of €2 is added.

Torino Card: This card is valid for 48 or 72 hours and gives free entrance to more than 130 museums, monuments, castles, fortresses and royal residences in Turin and Piedmont. It also gives free access to public transport, to the TurismoBus Torino, the panoramic lift in the Mole Antonelliana, to boats on the Po and to the rack tramway Sassi-Superga. It also offers many reductions on guided tours and some theatre and music shows. The Torino Card costs €16 for 48 hours or €18 for 72 hours and can be bought at Turismo Torino information points and in many Turin hotels.

Transport: Trams, buses and electric minibuses are operated by GTT (Gruppo Transporti Torinesi). A ticket, *ordinario urbano*, valid for 70 minutes for unlimited travel in the city, costs €0.90. A day pass, *giornaliero*, for unlimited travel in the city, costs €3. A ticket valid for 60 minutes' travel in the suburban area, *ordinario suburbano*, costs €0.90.

Youth hostel: €12–20 per person per night, excluding breakfast.

C

CAR HIRE (*autonoleggio*; see also DRIVING)

Driving in Turin is not recommended due to chronic traffic congestion and a lack of parking spaces. However, a car is almost a necessity for exploring the surrounding Piedmont region. All the major car-hire companies have agency windows in the arrivals area of the airport and are also listed in the yellow pages under 'Autonoleggio'.

You must be over 21 to hire a car (in some cases over 23 years old) and you need to have had a full driving licence for at least 12 months. Be sure to take a major credit card or a very substantial cash deposit, although cash is not always accepted. Check that the quoted rate includes collision damage waiver and personal accident insurance, unlimited mileage and tax, as these can greatly increase the cost.

I'd like to rent a car	**Vorrei noleggiare una macchina**
…for one day/a week.	**…per un giorno/una settimana.**
I want full insurance.	**Voglio l'assicurazione completa.**

CLIMATE

Turin has a continental climate, so summers are hot in the city and on the nearby plains, and pleasantly cool in the hills and mountains. Autumn and winter tend to be cold and the sun is frequently blotted out by haze and fog. The heaviest rainfall is from October to April, while the sunniest months are June, July and August. In Turin the hottest months are July and August, when temperatures can reach around 32°C (90°F).

	J	F	M	A	M	J	J	A	S	O	N	D
°C	6	8	13	17	21	25	28	27	23	17	11	7
°F	43	46	55	63	70	77	82	81	73	63	52	45

CLOTHING

Lightweight cotton and linen clothes are best for coping with the summer heat, but you'll want a sweater, fleece or jacket for the cool evenings in spring and autumn. In winter, you will need warm clothes, a waterproof jacket and an umbrella. Comfortable walking shoes are a must at any time of year.

At religious sites, dress respectably – shorts or bare shoulders are banned. If visiting the mountains (at any time of year), dress in layers and take some thermal clothing. If you intend to visit swimming pools, you must wear a bathing cap.

CRIME AND SAFETY

In general, Turin is a well-lit and safe place, but, in common with cities the world over, it is always advisable to be streetwise and to be especially vigilant for pickpockets. That said, at night it is best to avoid the areas west of Via Nizza around the station, Piazza Repubblica, the Murazzi and Parco Valentino, especially if you are on your own.

Although muggings are relatively rare, bag snatchers and pickpockets tend to haunt train and bus stations and markets. To prevent petty thieves from spoiling your trip, be sure to carry only the minimum cash needed and don't keep it in a back pocket. Keep all valuables such as credit cards and passport in a zipped pocket or money pouch inside your clothing and don't carry a camera or bag loosely slung over your street-side shoulder; wear them across the chest instead.

Scippatori, as motorbike thieves are known, are extraordinarily dexterous at relieving unsuspecting pedestrians of their valuables and are virtually impossible to catch. It's always a wise precaution to keep a photocopy of all your valuable documents, including passport and any travellers' cheques, in case of theft.

If you hire a car, never leave anything of value visible in the car when parked and, wherever possible, park in a garage or attended parking area. Always leave valuables that you don't need every day in the hotel safe. When travelling by train, keep the doors and windows of sleeping-car compartments locked at night.

If you are unlucky enough to be the victim of a crime, call the police helpline on 112 (English-speaking) or go to the nearest police station saying that you want to report a theft. A written statement *(denuncia)* will be drawn up for you, which you will need in order to make an insurance claim.

I want to report a theft.	**Voglio denunciare un furto.**
My wallet/passport/ticket has been stolen.	**Mi hanno rubato il portafoglio/il passaporto/ il biglietto.**

CUSTOMS AND ENTRY REQUIREMENTS

For a stay of up to three months, a valid passport is sufficient for citizens of Australia, Canada, New Zealand and the US. Visitors from the EU countries only need an identity card to enter Italy. Visitors from South Africa must have a visa. EU citizens don't have to declare goods exported from or imported into Italy so long as they come from another EU country. The import of narcotics, weapons and pirated materials is forbidden. Alcoholic drinks, tobacco and perfume may be imported in limited quantities, depending on your nationality and provided that the amount falls within what might be reasonably described as 'for personal use only'.

Currency restrictions. Tourists may bring an unlimited amount of euros or foreign currency into the country. There are no restrictions on the import of watches, cameras or electrical goods. On departure you must declare any currency beyond the equivalent of €10,000, so it's wise to declare sums exceeding this amount when you arrive.

Art. The Italian government is concerned about illegal traffic in works of art and archaeological relics. For such items you should obtain the correct receipts and documentation for export – *nulla oste* – from the dealer.

I've nothing to declare.	**Non ho niente da dichiarare.**
It's for my personal use.	**È per mio uso personale.**

D

DRIVING

Those planning to take their vehicle into Italy need a full driving licence, with Italian translation (or an international driving licence), an international motor insurance certificate and a vehicle registration document. A green insurance card (an extension to your ordinary insurance, making your policy valid for Italy) is strongly recommended.

The use of seat belts both in the front and back seats is obligatory and fines for non-compliance are stiff. Outside urban areas, you must drive with your headlights illuminated. A red warning triangle must be carried in case of breakdown. Note that, unlike in many countries, flashing your lights in Italy means that you will *not* slow down. Motorcycle riders must wear crash helmets.

For more information consult the ACI (Automobile Club d'Italia), tel: 011-57 791; in an emergency, tel: 116; for 24-hour information, tel: 803 116 or go to <www.acitorino.it>.

driving licence	**patente**
car registration papers	**libretto di circolazione**
Green Card	**carta verde**
I've had a breakdown.	**Ho avuto un guasto.**
There's been an accident.	**C'è stato un incidente.**

Driving conditions. Drive on the right and give way to traffic coming from the right. Speed limits are 50km/h (30mph) in town; 90km/h (55mph) on roads outside urban areas; 110km/h (70mph) on dual carriageways outside urban areas; 130km/h (80mph) on motorways *(autostrade)*. Nearly all charge tolls and you pay as you exit. On Alpine roads during winter you will need to fit chains or studded snow tyres. Call 1518 for an update on road conditions.

Are we on the right road for …?	**Siamo sulla strada giusta per …?**

Rules and regulations. The *polizia stradale* (traffic police) are very vigilant about imposing on-the-spot fines for speeding and other offences such as driving while intoxicated or stopping in a no-stopping zone. Hidden speed cameras are becoming very commonplace and, generally, police have become much stricter about speeding. All cities and many towns and villages have signs posted at the outskirts indicating the phone number of the local traffic police or *carabinieri*.

Fuel. *Benzina* (petrol) is unleaded *(senza piombo* or *verde)*; diesel is *gasolio*; liquid propane gas is GPL. Petrol stations are usually open 7am–12.30pm and 3–7.30pm, although many remain open throughout lunch nowadays and offer full service from pump attendants. Many are self-service (look for a '24' sign), and accept euro notes in various denominations and often credit/debit cards as well. Service stations on the *autostrade* are manned 24 hours a day.

Fill the tank please.	**Per favore, faccia il pieno de …**
super/normal	**super/normale**
lead-free/diesel	**senza piombo/gasolio**

Parking (*parcheggio*). Lack of parking makes taking a car into Turin a real challenge. Parking wardens are extremely vigilant and huge areas of the city, notably between Piazza Statuto and Piazza Castello, are closed to non-resident traffic 7.30–10.30am and additionally sometimes in the evening. From time to time, only cars with certain numberplates – usually odd or even numbers – are permitted to circulate in order to reduce congestion and pollution.

Parking areas marked by blue lines indicate that residents can park free and visitors pay. You pay between €0.50 and €2 per hour at pay-and-display meters and, for longer stays, you can buy parking cards for €30 from *tabacchi* which allow you to deduct the fees over a period of time. There are many no-parking zones, designated by signs such as *sosta vietata* – no parking; *passo carrabile* – access at all times; *zona rimozione* – tow-away area. Yellow stripes on the road designate disabled parking spaces.

Can I park here?	**Posso parcheggiare qui?**

Other areas have self-appointed guardians or *parcheggiatori* who, in theory, will make sure that your car is safe and doesn't have its tyres slashed – for a fee, of course. A much safer, though more expensive, option is to use one of the many underground car parks. In the event of not being able to find your car, it is highly likely that it has been towed away. Phone the municipal police (*vigili urbani*; tel: 011-812 3422 or 011-460 6060) to find out to which of the two car pounds it has been towed. Fines are hefty.

For more details of car-related restrictions visit the website <www.comune.torino.it>.

Road Signs. Most road signs in Italy are international. Here are some written signs you might come across:

Curva pericolosa	Dangerous bend/curve
Deviazione	Detour
Divieto di sorpasso	No overtaking
Divieto di sosta	No stopping
Pericolo	Danger
Rallentare	Slow down
Senso vietato/unico	No entry/One-way street
Vietato l'ingresso	No entry
Zona pedonale	Pedestrian zone
ZTL	Limited-traffic zone

E

ELECTRICITY *(elettricità)*

220v/50 Hz AC is standard. An adapter plug *(una presa complementare)* for continental-style sockets will be needed. American 110v appliances also need a voltage transformer *(un transformatore)* available from electrical appliance shops in Italy.

EMBASSIES AND CONSULATES *(ambasciate; consolati)*

In Turin:
UK (consulate): Via Madama Cristina 99, Turin, tel: 011-650 9202.

In Rome:
Australia (embassy): Via Alessandria 215, Rome, tel: 06-852 721, <www.australian-embassy.it>.
Canada (embassy): Via GB de Rossi 27, Rome, tel: 06-445 981, <www.canada.it>.
New Zealand (embassy): Via Zara 28, Rome, tel: 06-441 7171, <www.nzembassy.com>.
South Africa (embassy): Via Tanaro 14, Rome, tel: 06-852 541, <www.sudafrica.it>.

UK (embassy): Via XX Settembre 80ᵃ, Rome, tel: 06-4220 0001, <www.britain.it>.

US (embassy): Via Vittorio Veneto 119, Rome, tel: 06-46741, <www.usembassy.it>.

EMERGENCIES *(emergenza)*

Police (English-speaking helpline): **112**
General emergency (state police): **113**
Fire service: **115**
Ambulance: **118**
Car breakdown (ACI – Automobile Club d'Italia): **116**

Please can you place an emergency call to the …?	**Per favore, può fare una telefonata d'emergenza …?**
police	**alla polizia**
fire brigade	**ai vigili del fuoco**
hospital	**all'ospedale**

G

GAY AND LESBIAN TRAVELLERS

As a country, Catholic Italy has never been especially gay-friendly – at least not in the open. But of all the Italian cities, Turin has more gay, lesbian and transsexual associations than any other. Italy's first formal gay association outing had its national headquarters in Turin, called aptly enough *Fuori* (Out). The first national Gay Pride march was held here along with the first gay cinema festival, Da Sodoma a Hollywood, which is now internationally acclaimed and a permanent fixture. There are several good websites and help/information lines:

Circolo Maurice, Via della Basilica 5 (Piazza Castello), tel: 011-521 1116, <www.mauriceglbt.org>. A sports and social club with comprehensive listings of events.

Informagay, Via Giordano Bruno 80 (southern suburbs), tel: 011-304 0934, helpline 011-851 743 (Thur 8–11pm), <www.informa gay.it>. Good meeting place with information on upcoming events. Also offers counselling for gays, lesbians and transsexuals.

Other websites include <www.gay.it>, <www.arcigay.it> and <www.clubclassic.net/guida/torino_1.html>.

GETTING TO TURIN

By plane. Turin's Caselle airport is served daily by European carriers from most European cities. These include Alitalia, British Airways, Ryanair, Meridiana, AirDolomiti, Air France, Air One, Air Vallée, Austrian Airlines, SN Brussels Airlines, EasyJet, Finnair, Iberia, Lufthansa, Luxair, TAP Air Portugal and SAS. Turin is directly connected to many cities in the centre and south of Italy. In winter, charter flights from European cities add to this schedule, as Turin is a hub point for winter sports holidays.

By rail. Porta Nuova is the city's main railway station, offering international and national connections with Eurostar, Intercity, Inter-regional, Direct and Express trains. Fast trains operate from here to Milan (about 1 hour 20 minutes), Paris (under 5 hours) and many other European destinations. In 2008–9 Porta Nuova will lose its place as principal station to Porta Susa, which currently serves destinations north-west of the city and the Aosta Valley. For information on train timetables and fares contact TrenItalia (tel: 011-892 021, <www.trenitalia.com>). Train timetables can also be bought at any newsstand *(edicola)*.

single (one-way)	**andata**
return (round-trip)	**andata e ritorno**
first/second class	**prima/seconda classe**
What's the fare to …?	**Qual è la tariffa per …?**

By car. The Mont Blanc and Fréjus tunnels ensure good connections by road to countries north of the Alps. Paris is 765km (470 miles) away, while Lyon is 307km (190 miles). The A4 motorway linking Turin with Milan is fast, although at rush hour it is one of Italy's most congested *autostrade*.

By coach. You can travel to Turin directly by coach from many European cities. The trip from London takes around 24 hours. Eurolines run this service from London's Victoria Coach Station, tel: 08705-143 219, <www.eurolines.com>. The coach terminal in Turin is at the junction of Corso Inghilterra and Corso Vittorio Emanuele 11, tel: 011-433 2525.

GUIDES AND TOURS

Boat tours. Boat tours on the River Po are available during the summer months on the twin boats *Valentino* and *Valentina*. Both depart from the Murazzi quay.

Bus tours. The Turismo Bus Torino, operated by Turismo Torino, runs daily sightseeing tours during Easter, summer, Christmas and New Year, and at weekends during the rest of the year. Buses leave every hour and it's possible to hop off at any of the 14 stops and then rejoin the tour on the next bus. Tickets cost €6 per person (free for holders of the Torino Card) and can be bought on the bus, in any of Turismo Torino's three information points (Atrium Torino at Piazza Solferino, Porta Nuova station, Torino-Caselle airport) and in hotel.

Walking tours. Turismo Torino offers a range of English-language themed guided walking tours every Saturday at 6pm, such as 'Literary Turin' and 'Aperitif Under the Mole'. For information and bookings, tel: 011-535 181 or visit <www.turismotorino.org>. Tickets cost €7 (reductions for Torino Card holders).

H

HEALTH AND MEDICAL CARE

No vaccinations are required for entry into Italy. Visitors from EU countries carrying the E111 form (available from health centres or post offices before departure, and soon to be replaced with the European Health Insurance Card) are entitled to medical care under Italy's social security system. Non-European visitors should make sure they have health insurance. By law, hospital accident and emergency departments must treat all emergency cases free of charge. If you need to visit a doctor or dentist, your hotel or consulate should be able to recommend an English-speaking practitioner.

Pharmacies. In non-emergency cases it is worth remembering that pharmacists can often diagnose and prescribe medication for which at home you would normally need a doctor's prescription. Pharmacies display a green cross and normally follow shop hours and close for lunch. Addresses of pharmacies on duty at night or on public holidays appear on every chemist's door and in the local papers. The main night pharmacies in Turin are: Boniscontro, Corso Vittorio Emanuele 66 (near Porta Nuova station), Nizza, Via Nizza 65, and Comunale 21, Corso Belgio 151/b.

I need a doctor/a dentist.	**Ho bisogno di un medico/ dentista.**
Where's the nearest (all-night) chemist?	**Dov'è la farmacia (di turno) più vicina?**

HOLIDAYS

On public holidays, banks, government offices, most shops and some museums and galleries are closed. When a public holiday falls on a Thursday or Tuesday, Italians may make a *ponte* – bridge

– to the weekend, meaning that Friday or Monday is taken off as well. The most important holidays are:

1 January	Capodanno	New Year's Day
6 January	La Befana	Epiphany
Easter Monday	Pasquetta	
25 April	Festa della Liberazione	Liberation Day
1 May	Primo maggio, (also Festa del Lavoro)	Labour Day
2 June	Festa della Repubblica	Republic Day
24 June	San Giovanni	Patron saint of Turin's day
15 August	Ferragosto	Assumption Day
1 November	Tutti santi	All Saints' Day
8 December	Festa dell'Immacolata	Immaculate Conception
25 December	Natale	Christmas Day
26 December	Santo Stefano	Boxing Day

L

LANGUAGE

An effort to speak a little Italian will invariably be met with co-operation and smiles. Italians tend to be polite and will always use the traditional greetings of *buon giorno* (good morning) or *buona sera* (good evening) as a matter of course, even with strangers. The *Berlitz Italian Phrase Book & Dictionary* covers all the situations that you are likely to encounter in Italy. It also includes a pronunciation guide, basic grammar, and both English–Italian and Italian–English dictionaries.

M

MAPS

The Turismo Torino information point at Atrium2006, Piazza Solferino, is a good source of all information including maps.

Many maps of the area, including the excellent Touring Club of Italy maps, can be found at newsstands and bookshops.

MEDIA

Newspapers and Magazines (*giornali e riviste*). Newspapers and magazines in English are available at kiosks around Piazza Castello and Piazza San Carlo and at Porta Nuova station. The Luxembourg International Bookshop (Via Cesare Battisti 7) is a multilingual newsagent and bookshop. Turin's local newspaper is the national daily, *La Stampa*, part of the massive empire of Turin's Agnelli family. On Saturday it has a large colour supplement, *Specchio*, while on Friday it comes with *Torino Sette*, which has listings of cinema, music and other events.

Radio and TV (*radio, televisione*). There are seven major terrestrial television channels, three of which are owned by Silvio Berlusconi's Mediaset group. All programmes are in Italian, and, despite the great number of quiz and risqué chat shows involving various stages of undress, there are some good programmes, notably from the new Sky Italia, which has a wide range of channels. It is still quite rare to find films in their original version (*versione originale*) as most are dubbed into Italian. Most hotels and hired properties have cable or satellite which show CNN and BBC World, among others.

The three state-owned radio stations (RAI 1, 2 and 3) have a mix of chat, news, light and classical music. Generally the airwaves are crammed with stations mostly broadcasting pop and chart hits. Local Torinese stations include Radio Torino Popolare (97 FM), Radio Energy (93.9 FM), Radio Grp (99.3 FM) and Radio Flash (97.6 FM).

MONEY (*denaro*)

Italy's currency is the euro. Notes are in denominations of €5, 10, 20, 100, 200 and 500; coins are in €1 and 2 plus 1, 2, 5, 10, 20 and

50 cents *(centesimi)*. Notes and coins from any country in the Eurozone are legal tender in Italy.

Banks and bureaux de change *(banca; cambio)*. Banks give the best exchange rates. Don't forget to take along your passport when changing travellers' cheques. Bureaux de change are an alternative and have longer opening hours than banks, but commission rates vary widely.

Travellers' cheques. These can be used for purchases, but you will get much better value if you exchange your cheques for euros at a bank or a *cambio*. Passports are required when cashing cheques. Note that some smaller banks may not able to cash travellers' cheques.

I want to change some pounds/dollars/ travellers' cheques.	**Voglio cambiare delle sterline/dei dollari/ traveller cheque.**
Can I pay with this credit card?	**Posso pagare con la carta di credito?**
Where is the bank?	**Dov' è la banca?**

ATMs. Most banks have 24-hour ATMs *(bancomats)*.

Credit cards. Most hotels of two stars and above accept major credit cards, as do smarter restaurants; however, many tourist sites, basic restaurants/*trattorie*, small shops and market traders do not.

O

OPENING HOURS *(orari di aperture)*

Banks. Generally Mon–Fri 8.30am–1.30pm and 2.45–4.30pm. Some bigger branches in the centre stay open till 6pm on Thursdays and 8.30am–12.30pm on Saturdays.

Post offices. Mon–Sat 8.30am–1.30pm. The main post office at Via Alfieri 10 is open Mon–Fri 8.30am–7pm and Sat 8.30am–1pm.

Shops. While the traditional hours are Mon–Sat 9.30am–1pm and 3.30–7.30pm, many shops now stay open for lunch and some stay open later in the evening and even on Sunday. Food shops are usually closed on Wednesday afternoons and most non-food shops close on Monday mornings.

Tourist sites. Almost all museums and galleries close on Monday. However, most churches are open and several markets, including Porta Palazzo, do a roaring trade on this day.

P

POLICE

The main police station, Questura, is at Corso Vinzaglio 10, tel: 011-558 81. This deals with complaints and is a good point of reference should you need help from the authorities. The *carabinieri* – who maintain law and order throughout the country – are at Via Santa Croce 6, tel: 011-6881.

In an emergency dial 112 for police assistance.

Where's the nearest police station?	**Dov' è il commissariato di polizia più vicino?**

POST OFFICES (*posta*)

Post offices are designated by the yellow sign with PT in black. Normal post office hours are Mon–Sat 8.30am–1.30pm. The main post office at Via Alfieri 10 is open Mon–Fri 8.30am–7pm and Sat 8.30am–1pm (tel: 011-803 160). The *posta prioritaria* is equivalent to first-class post and usually works well, promising delivery within one day in Italy, three days for EU countries and up to five for the rest of the world. A first-class stamp for any EU country costs €0.62 and €0.41 for a postcard. Postcards tend to arrive more quickly when put in an envelope.

Where's the nearest post office?	**Dov' è l' ufficio postale più vicino?**
A stamp for this letter/ postcard, please.	**Un francobollo per questa lettera/cartolina' per favore.**

PUBLIC TRANSPORT (see also BUDGETING FOR YOUR TRIP)

Buses and trams. Turin has an efficient, value-for-money network of buses and trams run by GTT (Gruppo Torinesi Trasporti), tel: 800-019 152, <www.gtt.to.it>, which has a sales office in the Porta Nuova atrium. The network operates from 5am till midnight and tickets are transferable between tram and bus. Tickets can be bought at *tabacchi*. The Torino Card, available from Tourismo Torino and hotels, gives free access to public transport.

Metro *(la metropolitana)*. Turin is in the process of building a metro system. The line Porta Nuova–Lingotto is due to be ready for the Winter Olympics in 2006. Inevitably, while so much work is in progress, many buses and trams have been rerouted, so the best advice during this period of change is to arm yourself with the most up-to-date route map possible, available from tourist information outlets, tobacconists and newsagents.

Taxis. To find a taxi, go to a taxi rank or order one by telephone – it is not customary to hail them in the street. Authorised taxis are white in colour and have the city's emblem on the rear licence plate and front doors. Ranks are signalled by 'taxi' written in black on an orange sign. If you call for a taxi you will be charged for the distance/time that it takes to come to pick you up, plus the fare. When your call is answered, you will be given the taxi code-name and a time. Three recommended companies are: Pronto Taxi (tel: 011-5737); Radio Taxi (tel: 011-3399/5730); and CTA (tel/fax: 011-996 3090). It is useful to have a fistful of change ready as taxi drivers are notorious for rounding up the fare.

Trains. There are three stations. The Porta Nuova is the main terminus in the heart of the city, Porta Susa lies in the northwest, and the small Dora station is linked to the airport. Note, however, that Porta Susa is due to replace Porta Nuova as the main station in 2008–09.

Italian trains are classified according to speed. The fastest and best are Eurostar Italia (ES), which cost more than double the slower trains. Advance reservation on this service is obligatory. The Inter-City (IC) and EuroCity services are also fast and cost up to 50 percent more than the slower trains and should be booked in advance also. The slower trains – the *diretto*, *espresso*, *regionale* and *interregionale* – stop more frequently but are very cheap. The universal phone number for all Italian stations is 892 021. For details of all fares and timetable information go to <www.trenitalia.com> or buy a timetable from any newsstand. Remember that you must stamp your ticket in one of the machines on the station platform before travelling, otherwise you could be subject to a hefty fine.

When's the next bus/ train/boat/plane for…?	**A che ore parte il prossimo autobus/treno/traghetto/ aereo per...?**
What's the fare to...?	**Quanto costa il biglietto per...?**
I want a ticket to...	**Vorrei un biglietto per...**
single (one-way)	**andata**
return (round-trip)	**andata e ritorno**
first/second class	**prima/seconda classe**
I'd like to make seat reservations.	**Vorrei prenotare un posto.**

R

RELIGION

There are over 200 Roman Catholic churches in Turin, but none
has Mass in English. Of the other denominations, the Evangelical
church of Casa Valdese (Corso Vittorio Emanuele II 23, tel: 011-
669 2838) has services in English at 10.30am on Sunday.

S

SMOKING

Smoking in public places, including most bars and restaurants, is
against the law. The law allows smoking in bars and restaurants that
have special air-conditioned rooms for smokers. Note that many Italians are sceptical of a prohibitionism which they feel smacks of American or northern European Puritanism.

T

TELEPHONE

As well as public telephones, you can use phones in bars and cafés,
indicated by an orange telephone sign outside. Most public telephones only accept phone cards (*schede telefoniche*) which are
available in various denominations from tobacconists and Telecom
Italia offices. When dialling in Turin, land-line numbers begin with
the area code 011 and this must be used regardless of whether you
are calling inside or outside the city. For international calls dial 00,
followed by the appropriate country code – e.g. UK is 44. For calls
to the UK omit the initial zero of the area code, then follow with the
number. For operator and Italian directory enquiries dial 12; for the
International Operator dial 170; for International Directory Enquiries dial 4176. Hotels tend to charge very high sums for direct
calls and often add service charges for toll-free calls on their line.

In this land where mobile phones are not just an accessory but a fashion necessity, it's as well to remember that mobile phone numbers now begin with 3 (until recently it was 03, but the zero is now redundant).

TICKETS

Advance tickets for performances and events can often be purchased through the concierge in better hotels. The Torino Card *(see page 108)* is an invaluable tool for free entrance to museums, galleries, etc in and around Turin and also gives reductions of up to 40 percent on theatre performances and concerts.

TIME ZONE

Italy follows Central European Time (GMT+1). From late March to the last weekend in October clocks are put forward one hour.

Vancouver	New York	London	**Turin**	Jo'burg	Sydney
3am	6am	11am	**noon**	1pm	8pm

TIPPING

While Italians do not generally go overboard on tipping, it is generally expected from foreign visitors. Most of the larger restaurants include a 10–15 percent service charge, and it is customary to give the waiter something extra, preferably in cash and around 10 percent of the bill. Usually, tipping is not expected in family-run restaurants, but a few euros are always appreciated. Porters, barmen, doormen and service-station attendants all expect a tip, as do taxi drivers who will be appreciative if you round up the taxi fare.

Thank you, this is for you.	**Grazie, questo è per lei.**
Keep the change.	**Tenga il resto.**

TOILETS

It is important not to confuse the wording on lavatory doors. Straightforward as *Uomini* might be for men and *Donne* for women, confusion can and often does occur between *Signori* for men and *Signore* for women. Toilets in bars are not always clean and quite a few are still a hole in the floor. Larger hotels are a good bet, as are most major tourist sites, where there are usually attendants who will expect a small tip.

Where are the toilets?	**Dove sono i gabinetti?**

TOURIST INFORMATION

Turin's main tourist information centre is in the Atrium2006 at Piazza Solferino (open daily 9.30am–7pm). Also here is the Vetrina Torino Cultura which gives information on shows and cultural events. Other locations are Porta Nuova station by platform 17 (open Mon–Sat 9.30am–7pm and Sun until 3pm) and Turin-Caselle airport arrivals hall (open daily 8.30am–10.30pm). You can call Turismo Torino on tel: 011-535 181 or view their website at <www.turismotorino.org>.

Within Piedmont, every major town has an Azienda di Promozione Turistica (APT) or Informazione e Accoglienza Turistica (IAT). Both organisations are operated by the Italian State Tourist Offices, <www.enit.it>, which gives information on locations of tourist offices in Italy and abroad.

Where's the tourist office?	**Dov'è l'ufficio turistico?**

W

WEIGHTS AND MEASURES

Italy uses the metric system.

Recommended Hotels

The Italian government rates hotels from one star to 'five star L' (luxury). These ratings are based purely on amenities provided – not on quality of service or ambience. In comparison with other major Italian cities, there are fewer five-star hotels in Turin; however, there is a wide range of accommodation available, from designer to budget.

Prices in Turin tend to be lower than in Milan, Rome, Venice and Florence, but reservations need to be made well in advance. Normally, rates are generally lower in winter than at other times. Some hotels catering predominantly to business clients offer good discounts throughout the year for weekend stays, when they have spare capacity.

The prices below indicate room rates per night for a double room. Most budget and moderately priced hotels include breakfast in the room rate, but, as a general rule, the more expensive the hotel the less likely that breakfast is included. Older hotels tend not to have wheelchair access; contact an establishment directly if this is a requirement. For more information on accommodation, *see page 106.*

€€€€	250 euros and above
€€€	180–250 euros
€€	125–180 euros
€	under 125 euros

TURIN

Ai Savoia € *Via del Carmine 1/B; tel: 339-125 7711; <www.aisavoia.it>*. Reasonably priced, welcoming B&B just off the quiet Piazza Savoie in the Quadrilatero Romano. The rooms are comfortable with baroque flourishes.

Bologna € *Corso Vittorio Emanuele II 60; tel: 011-562 0191; fax: 011-562 0193; <www.hotelbolognasrl.it>*. This friendly, family-run budget hotel, which opened in 1899, is next to the Porta Nuova station and gives a warm welcome. Most rooms here have new bathrooms, soft lighting, parquet floors and modern furniture.

Boston €€€ *Via Massena 70; tel: 011-500 359; fax: 011-599 358; <www.hotelbostontorino.it>*. Located in the Crocetta district, this four-star hotel occupies two buildings, one of which is an excellent example of the Liberty style. The interior has been tastefully renovated with great attention to comfort. In the public rooms on the ground floor there is an impressive display of the owner's art collection, which blends works by American artists, such as Lichtenstein and Warhol, with Italian artists. In fact, the hotel's motto is 'the hotel of art, the art of the hotel'. The newer rooms have oriental *objets d'art* but the overall effect is modern minimalist. Unusually for Turin, this hotel has a small garden.

City €€€–€€€€ *Via Juvarra 25; tel: 011-540 546; fax: 011-548 188; <www.bwhotelcity-to.it>*. Highly individual, contemporary décor and striking art are the delights of this four-star hotel with 57 rooms. Conveniently sited near the Porta Susa railway station, the hotel looks across to a quiet garden from bedrooms which are well equipped, with many personal touches. No restaurant.

Des Artistes €€€ *Via Principe Amedeo 21; tel: 011-812 4416; fax: 011-812 4466; <www.desartisteshotel.it>*. This recently renovated central hotel is close to the Piazza Vittorio Veneto with all its restaurants and bars. The 22 rooms are quiet, comfortable and well appointed, and service is polite and professional. As the name suggests, it has a certain bohemian air.

Diplomatic €€€–€€€€ *Via Cernaia 42; tel: 011-561 2444; fax: 011-540 472; <www.hotel-diplomatic.it>*. Close to the Porta Susa station, this six-storey building nestles underneath the porticoed walkways in one of the city's most elegant streets. The interior is modern and stylish and, while the bedrooms are not large, they afford a high standard of comfort. This 126-bedroom hotel also has conference facilities.

Genio €€€ *Corso Vittorio Emanuele II 47; tel: 011-650 5771; fax: 011-650 8264; <www.hotelgenio.it>.* A good three-star, recently renovated hotel, conveniently situated near the Porta Nuova station. There is good attention to detail in most of the 120 rooms with pleasing co-ordinated fabrics. No restaurant, but there is the bonus of a private garage.

Genova e Stazione €€€ *Via Sacchi 14B; tel: 011-562 9400; fax: 011-562 9896; <www.albergogenova.it>.* A member of the Best Western group, this well-priced hotel close to the Porta Nuova railway station has all modern comforts within a beautiful 19th-century building. The décor features chandeliers, mirrors and painted ceilings. The bedrooms on the top floor have great rooftop views.

Gilda B&B € *1 Via S. Bernardino 12; tel: 011-375 241; <www. bbgilda.it>.* Three rooms are available in this B&B in the lively area of Borgo San Paolo, southwest of the city centre. Clean, comfortable and modestly priced.

Grand Hotel Sitea €€–€€€€ *Via Carlo Alberto 35; tel: 011-517 0171; fax: 011-548 090; <www.thi.it>.* Located behind Piazza San Carlo, this historic hotel is convenient for the Via Roma and the railway station. It is atmospheric in its classic décor in the grand style, with wood panelling and elegant furnishings. The bathrooms are of marble and some have Jacuzzis. It is popular with celebrities and its elegant restaurant, the Carignano, is noted for the excellence of its food.

Le Meridien Art + Tech €€€€ *Via Nizza 230, Lingotto; tel: 011-664 2000; fax: 011-664 2001; <www.lemeridien-lingotto.it>.* This five-star hotel is a monument to cutting-edge design; style gurus Philippe Starck, Antonio Citterio and Giò Ponti have all left their mark. In the bedrooms plasma-screen televisions and exhilarating power-showers are standard, as are allergy-free bed linen and carpets. From the jogging track on the roof there are glorious, panoramic views of the Alps. The glass-roofed central hall has three fast glass lifts.

Le Meridien Lingotto €€€€ *Via Nizza 262; tel: 011-664 2000; fax: 011-664 2001; <www.lemeridien-lingotto.it>*. In the Lingotto centre, which was once part of the old Fiat factory, this Renzo Piano-designed hotel is ultra minimalist but with a tropical garden at its heart. The bedrooms are spacious with design artefacts and walls made entirely of glass. Although it is out of the centre of town, the facilities in the adjoining Lingotto complex make this like a little city within a city.

Montevecchio € *Via Montevecchio 13; tel: 011-562 0023; fax: 011-562 3047; <www.hotelmontevecchio.com>*. Modest and very friendly, this small hotel is just a stone's throw south of Porta Nuova station. The bedrooms, although basic, are bright and colourful and very comfortable.

Ostello Torino € *Via Alby 1; tel: 011-660 2939; fax: 011-660 4445; <www.ostellionline.org>*. The city's youth hostel is on the 'Collina' across the River Po near Piazza Crimea. There are 76 beds, and rooms sleep up to a maximum of six, although there are two family rooms with en-suite facilities. Rooms are clean and quiet. Meals are available.

Piemontese €€€ *Via Berthollet 21; tel: 011-669 8101; fax: 011-669 0571; <www.hotelpiemontese.it>*. Located between the Porta Nuova station and the River Po, this pleasant three-star hotel in a 19th-century Liberty-style building has just 37 rooms. The bedrooms are constantly being upgraded and some feature hydro-massage baths. No restaurant.

Starhotel Majestic €€€ *Corso Vittorio Emanuele II 54; tel: 011-539 153; fax: 011-534 963; <www.starhotels.com>*. Close to Porta Nuova station, this totally renovated, elegant hotel is like a 19th-century town house. A tall glass cupola creates a grand atmosphere in the restaurant, which serves local and international cuisine, and the 122 rooms are spacious and very well appointed. The hotel is a favourite with business clients and upmarket tour groups, as well as with independent travellers who find the atmosphere both stylish and comfortable.

Statuto € *Via Principi d'Acaja 17; tel: 011-434 4638; fax: 011-434 4380.* Located just off Corso Francia, a few streets west of the Porta Susa station, this family-run budget hotel is basic but very comfortable. Good buffet breakfasts.

Turin Palace Hotel €€€–€€€€ *Via Sacchi 8; tel: 011-562 5511; fax: 011-561 2187; <www.thi.it>.* This four-star hotel, sister to the Grand Hotel Sitea *(see page 131)*, is centrally located next to Porta Nuova station. Since its opening in 1872 in a converted 19th-century palazzo, it has been one of Turin's top establishments and has an air of traditional old charm. It's a long-time favourite with visiting celebrities.

Victoria €€–€€€ *Via Nino Costa 4; tel: 011-561 1909; fax: 011-561 1806; <www.hotelvictoria-torino.com>.* This hotel has few rivals for atmosphere, fascination and excellent service at three-star prices. It is rather like stepping into an English country house full of antiques and *objets d'art* collected by the owners on their travels far and wide. Each of the spacious 100 bedrooms is individually and pleasingly decorated, while downstairs there is an open fire and bar and a very pleasant conservatory-style breakfast room; in summer, breakfast is served in the garden under the gazebo. The hotel is centrally situated, very close to Piazza San Carlo and Via Roma. Not surprisingly, it attracts a faithful following and tends to get full very quickly.

Villa Sassi €€€ *Strada Traforo del Pino 47; tel: 011-898 0556; fax: 011-898 0095; <www.villasassi.com>.* Located a little way out of town, just below the Basilica di Superga, this four-star hotel is pleasantly set in large grounds. A former 17th-century villa, it is furnished with fine antiques, has an elegant restaurant and enjoys a peaceful location away from the hubbub of the city.

ASTI

Hotel Reale €–€€ *Piazza Alfieri 6; tel: 0141-530 240; fax: 0141-343 57; <www.hotel-reale.com>.* This lovely palazzo in the heart of Asti's old town has been a hotel since 1793. The reception

area and the 24 bedrooms, some of which are very spacious, are
tastefully decorated. No restaurant.

ALBA

Agriturismo Villa La Meridiana Cà Reiné *Località Altavilla 9
(1km east of Alba on the road to Altavilla); tel/fax: 0173-440 112.*
This elegant Liberty-style villa is the perfect spot for lovers of
peace and quiet. From the grounds, there are magnificent views of
the red-tiled roofs and towers of the town below, with the Langhe
and Alps in the background. The villa has four rooms and four mini
apartments with cooking facilities. Special attractions include a traditional grape diet during the harvest and, in the autumn, truffle
searches can be organised on the estate.

I Castelli €–€€ *Corso Torino 14; tel: 0173-361 978; fax: 0173-361
974; <www.hotel-icastelli.com>.* Opened in 1996, this modern
hotel built of cement and glass is in the centre of town, just 500m
(550yds) from the cathedral. Bedrooms are spacious, sound-proofed
and elegantly furnished. Covered parking facilities are included.

Hotel Savona € *Via Roma 1; tel: 0173-440 440; fax: 0173-363
475; <www.hotelsavona.com>.* This three-star hotel in the centre
of town has upheld the area's finest traditions in hospitality for over
100 years. Every modern comfort is offered. The restaurant specialises in local and regional specialities (including truffles) and the
café does great *aperitivi*. Parking in the garage available.

CANELLI

Agriturismo La Casa in Collina *Località Sant'Antonio 30
(2km/1 mile west of Canelli; 29km/18miles from Asti); tel: 0141-
822827; fax: 0141-823543.* As its name suggests, this lovely house
sits on a hill, overlooking vineyards, and enjoys stunning views of
the snowy peaks of the Alps in the distance. There are six spacious
and very comfortable rooms furnished with period pieces and
antiques, and the views from the breakfast room are simply breathtaking. The family is most hospitable and welcoming.

BRA

Albergo dell'Agenzia €€€ *Via Fossano 21, Pollenzo, Bra (7km/ 4 miles south-east of Bra); tel: 0172-458 600; fax: 0172-458 645; <www. albergoagenzia.it>*. Set in the premises of the University of Gastronomic Sciences, this four-star hotel is housed in part of what was once King Carlo Alberto's neo-Gothic residence. The 47 rooms are extremely spacious and elegantly furnished and each bears the name of a famous vineyard of Barolo, Barbaresco and Roero, underlining the strong link between the area and its culture, faithful to the philosophy of the Slow Food Movement.

BAROLO

La Terrazza sul Bosco € *Via Conforso 5; tel: 0173-561 37; fax: 0173-560 812.* Lying at the foot of the Marchesi Falletti castle, this *agriturismo* has five rooms – the same number as the wines made on the farm. A typical Piedmontese country home belonging to the Camerano family of vine-growers, it dates back to the 17th century and has splendid views from the lovely terrace out onto the 'Fava' wood – hence the name.

ALAGNA

Residence Mirella €–€€ *Fraz. Bonda; tel/fax: 0163-922 965.* Close to the church in the centre of this beautiful mountain village, the Residence is a charming, family-run affair. The cosy rooms are quite basic but have kitchenettes, and downstairs there is a friendly bar which serves breakfast (additional charge).

SESTRIERE

Miramonti *Via Cesana 3; tel: 0122-755 333; fax: 0122-755 375; <www.miramontisestriere.com>*. This family-run hotel has an enviable position next to the ski slopes and a golf course. The spacious 30 bedrooms are clad in wood and are both intimate and welcoming. The glass-clad breakfast room and terraces have beautiful mountain views.

Recommended Restaurants

Turin has some excellent restaurants that are also extremely good value. If you are travelling beyond the city, try some of the out-of-town restaurants for excellent Piedmontese cuisine; these places often also have beautiful views.

Many restaurants close for part of at least one day during the week – often on a Monday or Tuesday evening. Lunch is usually served from 12.30 to 3pm, when the kitchens close promptly, while dinner is from around 7.30 or 8pm, and last orders from the kitchen are at about 11pm, although *osterie* and cafés stay open later till around 1am. Trade shows and important events such as the Salone del Gusto attract many gourmets, so, whenever possible, make reservations. Most restaurants have banned smoking indoors. In summer, restaurants offering al fresco dining generally allow smoking outdoors.

The following listings cover a three-course meal, cover and service charges, but not wine or any gratuities. Ranges are given as guides only. It is worth noting that the fine tradition of the *aperitivi* in Turin means that many people never make it to dinner, which is a pity. Also listed under Turin are recommended bars and cafés for sampling *aperitivi*.

€€€	50 euros and up
€€	25–40 euros
€	25 euros or below

TURIN

RESTAURANTS

L'Agrifoglio €€ *Via Accademia Albertina 38/D; tel: 011-837 064.* In the heart of the city, close to Piazza Carlo Emanuele II, this trattoria is modern, small and intimate. It specialises in seasonal produce and is especially noted for wild mushrooms, truffles and game. Dinner only. Closed Sunday and Monday (except in July).

Al Garamond €€–€€€ *Via Pomba 14; tel: 011-812 2781*. This elegant restaurant in the heart of the city serves creative modern cuisine. Antipasti are a speciality and set menus featuring either fish or meat, or both together such as fish carpaccio with foie gras, are excellent value. Home-made bread and delicious puddings are also very tempting. As one of Turin's best-loved restaurants, booking is strongly recommended. Closed Saturday lunchtime and Sunday.

Antiche Sere €–€€ *Via Cenischia 9; tel: 011-385 4347*. There is a very welcoming atmosphere in this typical Torinese *osteria*, which is out of the centre, close to the Corso Racconigi. Regional favourites feature such as *vitello tonnato* and *stinco di maiale*, all made with the freshest ingredients. Service is very friendly and, as it is very popular with locals, it is advisable to book. Closed Sunday, August and Christmas.

Arcadia € *Galleria Subalpina 16, Piazza Castello; tel: 011-561 3898*. Choose between traditional Piedmontese cuisine and sushi in this buzzing central restaurant. Tempura and udon are served at the bar while the surrounding tables concentrate on Italian fare. Open for lunch and dinner. Closed Sunday.

Casa Vicina €€€ *Via Massena 66; tel: 011-590 949*. Close to Porta Nuova station, this well-regarded family restaurant produces modern, light versions of traditional Piedmontese specialities. Dinner only. Closed Sunday, Monday and July.

C'era Una Volta €€ *Corso Vittorio Emanuele II 41; tel: 011-655 498*. Close to Porta Nuova station, this well-established restaurant serves classical Piedmontese cuisine but with light touches too. Risotto with cheese and truffles, little puff pastry tarts with porcini mushrooms and wild boar feature. There is also an excellent *menu degustazione*. Dinner only. Closed Sunday and August.

Locanda Mongreno €€€ *Strada Mongreno 50; tel: 011-898 0417*. This former *osteria* in the hills of Turin has been transformed into a romantic, very stylish Michelin-starred restaurant. The cuisine is creative, light and highly imaginative, although the more hearty Piedmontese specialities also feature, such as *agnolotti*. There's an extensive cheese board and delicious puddings, many of which are chocolate based. For the sweet-toothed try *I cinque gusti* – a selection of five heavenly creations. Dinner only. Closed Monday, Christmas and late August–early September.

Mina €€ *Via Ellero 36; tel: 011-696 3608.* This popular, elegant restaurant takes its name from its owner. Its speciality is Piedmontese cuisine made with fresh, seasonal produce. Although out of the centre of town, south of Porta Nuova station, it is nonetheless advisable to book. Closed Sunday evening, Monday, mid-June–early July, and August.

La Pista €€€ *Via Nizza 262 (pedestrian entrance), Via Nizza 294 (entrance by car which takes you up the amazing spiral ramp), Lingotto; tel: 011-631 3523.* Named after the rooftop car test track on top of the Lingotto centre, this elegant restaurant has spectacular views over the city framed by the Alps in the distance. The food is excellent with traditional Piedmontese dishes alongside creative delicacies and a well-chosen wine list. Booking essential. Closed one week in January and three weeks in August.

Ristorante del Cambio €€€ *Piazza Carignano 2; tel: 011-543 760.* Established in 1757, this is Turin's most famous restaurant and its grand tradition is reflected in its excellent Piedmontese cuisine. For carniviores, this is the place to sample the authentic *bollito misto* – seven or more different meats served with seven sauces, reflecting the magical properties of that number. But every taste is catered for and lighter dishes feature together with sublime puddings and delicious little *bônets* – amaretto biscuits dipped in dark chocolate – with your coffee. Service is faultless and the wine list is long on Piedmontese reds as well as other Italian and international wines. Booking essential. Closed Sunday, first week of January and mid-August. (Thursday lunch is devoted to a tasting of *bollito misto*.)

Savoia €€–€€€ *Via Corte D'Appello 13; tel: 011-436 2288.* This well-established, elegant restaurant in the fashionable Quadrilatero

Romano offers set menus, including a small traditional one for those with less hearty appetites, as well as à la carte. Fish and vegetarian options feature, as well as classic Piedmontese meat dishes. The high standards of service and cuisine, together with a reasonably priced wine list, make this a very popular restaurant, so booking is recommended. Closed Saturday lunchtime and Sunday.

Sotto La Mole €€ *Via Montebello 9; tel: 011-817 9398.* Opposite the Museo Nazionale del Cinema, overlooked by the Mole Antonelliana, this brick-vaulted little restaurant is very popular. Lovers of offal will be in their element, but if that is not to your taste there are plenty of Piedmontese classical and innovative dishes to tantalise the taste buds. Booking advised. Dinner only (except Sunday). Closed Wednesday, three weekends in June, and Christmas.

Trattoria Mamma Licia € *Via Mazzini 50; tel: 011-888 942.* This friendly, family-run central trattoria, close to the Piazza Cavour, specialises in traditional Piedmontese home cooking. Delicious antipasti are served up on overflowing plates and each table has a 2-litre *pintone* of Barbera wine, which flows all too easily (you are charged according to what you have consumed). Mains include classics such as *stinco di maiale*. Try to leave room for excellent local cheeses and desserts. Dinner only. Closed Sunday.

Tre Galline €€–€€€ *Via Bellezia 37; tel: 011-436 6553.* Set in the Quadrilatero, this famous restaurant is also one of Turin's oldest and best loved, offering great food at very reasonable prices. Excellent traditional Piedmontese cuisine features, and each evening a different local speciality is on offer – such as *bollito misto*, served from a trolley groaning under the weight of so many mixed meats. Lighter dishes also feature and the wine list is extensive and good value. Closed Monday lunchtime, Sunday, early January and mid-August.

Le Vitel Etonné €–€€ *Via San Francesco da Paola 4; tel: 011-812 4621.* Very close to Piazza Castello, this is a buzzing *vineria* cum restaurant. Perfect for a glass of wine and nibbles, for a light lunch or full dinner, the menu changes daily but, faithful to its name, always features *vitello tonnato*. A spiral staircase leads down to the atmospheric wine cellar. Closed Wednesday and Sunday evening.

BARS AND CAFÉS

Il Bacaro *Piazza della Consolata*. Wine bar overlooking the tranquil Piazza della Consolata.

La Drogheria *Piazza Vittorio Veneto 18D*. A new bar on the very popular Piazza Vittorio. There's a fun, buzzing atmosphere in several different rooms.

Caffè Elena *Piazza Vittorio Veneto 5*. Once Nietzsche's favourite haunt, now very popular with students and literary types.

Hafa Café *Via Sant'Agostino 23c*. A little piece of Morocco serving exotic Mahgreb *aperitivi*.

Lab Night/Day *Piazza Vittorio Veneto 13*. Contemporary bar very popular with the Torinesi and bright young things.

Mood Libri & Caffè *Via Cesare Battisti 3/e*. A bar cum bookshop where the motto is 'moments out of duty'. Relaxed, literary crowd and excellent *aperitivi*.

Caffè Norman *Via Pietro Micca 22*. Sumptuous surroundings and lavish buffets.

Platti *Corso Vittorio Emanuele 72*. The lovely Liberty design is as stylish as the clientele and as sumptuous as the choice of *aperitivi*.

Caffè Roberto *Via Po 5*. Huge banquets are served in this elegant café under the porticoed Via Po.

SFASHIONcafè *Via Cesare Battisti 13*. Owned by TV personality, Chiambretti, this retro café is full of cartoons and murals. Nietzsche used to live two floors above.

RIVOLI

Combal.zero €€€ *Piazza Mafalda di Savoia; tel: 011-956 5225.*
This highly acclaimed restaurant (the proud holder of a Michelin
star) continues its tradition of creative, innovative gourmet cuisine.
Specialities include fish with black truffles, foie gras, beef – especially *gelatina di manzo al Porto*. Excellent service.

ASTI

L'Angolo del Beato €€ *Via Guttuari 12; tel: 0141-531 668.* This
family-run little restaurant has a very discreet entrance, but once
inside it is like going into someone's home. The decor has a distinct
French touch and the cuisine relies heavily on the regional and seasonal. Rabbit is often on the menu – perhaps in a tuna sauce – along
with peppers with *bagna cauda*, and delicious zabaglione with
Moscato d'Asti also feature. Closed Sunday, Christmas and first
three weeks in August.

ALBA

Daniel's Al Pesco Fiorito €€ *Corso Canale 28 (1km/under 1 mile
north-west of Alba); tel: 0173-441 977.* The flowering peach tree
(pesco) is a symbol of the Roero region and this restaurant is at the
gateway to this lovely hilly area. Typical Alba cuisine with creative
touches is served here in the elegant dining room. The wine cellar is
well stocked with top-quality local Piedmontese wines, and there is a
huge selection of grappas. Closed Sunday (except in the truffle season, September–November), Christmas and late July–mid-August.

Locanda del Pilone €€€ *Frazione Madonna di Como 34 (5km/
3 miles south-east of Alba); tel: 0173-366 616.* Overlooking hills
and vineyards, this Michelin-starred restaurant specialises in local
cuisine. In autumn the *crema al parmigiano e tartufo bianco d'Alba*
(parmesan and white truffle soup) is sublime. Another treat is the
white chocolate mousse. There are also six rooms here if the
gourmet experience overwhelms you. Book essential. Closed Tuesday and Wednesday lunchtime, Christmas and late July–late August.

BAROLO

Locanda nel Borgo Antico €€€ *Piazza Municipio 2; tel: 0173-56355.* This acclaimed restaurant in a country nobleman's house in Barolo's old centre serves creative Piedmontese cuisine. In the hazelnut season you might see *tortino caldo di nocciola tonda gentile alla crema di moscato* – warm hazelnut tart with moscato. Closed Tuesday, Wednesday lunchtime (except October–November), six weeks from early January, and two weeks in August.

BRA

La Corte Albertina €€ *Piazza Vittorio Emanuele 3 (in Pollenzo, 7km/4 miles south-east of Bra); tel: 0172-458 189.* Set in the 18th-century portico of a farm that once belonged to the Savoy family, this atmospheric restaurant still has original beams and other features. Original recipes favoured by Carlo Alberto are on the menu, including mountain-stream trout and pheasant. Try to keep room for delicious puddings such as the *tortino di cioccolato fondente* – a chocolate confection that melts in the mouth. Closed Wednesday and Sunday evening, and January.

BARDONECCHIA

Locanda Biovey €€ *Via General Cantore 2; tel: 0122-999 215.* This little restaurant with rooms is in a former *palazzo* and serves creative cuisine based on traditional Piedmontese fare. Cheese soufflés, venison carpaccio and chocolate puddings all feature. Closed Tuesday and in low season; also Monday evening. Closed for three weeks in May and October.

SESTRIERE

Du Grand Pere €€ *Via Forte Seguin 14 (5km/3 miles south-west of Sestriere), Champlas-Janvier; tel: 0122-755 970.* Rustic, atmospheric restaurant in a 17th-century house. The cuisine includes seasonal produce such as game and authentic mountain fare. Open December–April, and mid-June–mid-September. Closed Tuesday.

INDEX